346.7301 Ste
Stewart, James W. (James
The child custody book :
how to protect your   *2004*

DUUK

The
Child
Custody
Book

How to Protect Your Children and Win Your Case

Judge James W. Stewart

With contributions from Terry Johnston, Ph.D.,
Licensed Psychologist, Custody Evaluator

Impact Publishers, Inc.
ATASCADERO, CALIFORNIA

ATTENTION ORGANIZATIONS AND CORPORATIONS:
This book is available at quantity discounts on bulk purchases for educational, business, or sales promotional use. For further information, please contact Impact Publishers, P.O. Box 6016, Atascadero, CA 93423-6016, Phone: 1-800-246-7228. E-mail: sales@impactpublishers.com

---

Library of Congress Cataloging-in-Publication Data

Stewart, James W. (James Webster)
    The child custody book : how to protect your children and win your case /
James W. Stewart.
      p.cm. -- (Rebuilding books, for divorce and beyond)
    Includes index.
    ISBN 1-886230-27-7 (alk. paper)
    1. Custody of children--Unied States. I. Title. II. Series.
KF547.Z9 S745 2000
346.7301'73--dc21

                        99-089891

Publishers' Note
This publication is designed to provide accurate and authoritative information in regard to the subject matter covered. It is sold with the understanding that the publisher is not engaged in rendering psychological, legal, or other professional services. If expert assistance or counseling is needed, the services of a competent professional should be sought.

Impact Publishers and colophon are registered trademarks of Impact Publishers, Inc.

Cover design by Sharon Schnare, San Luis Obispo, California.
Printed in the United States of America on acid-free paper,
Published by **Impact✒ Publishers, Inc.**
POST OFFICE BOX 6016
ATASCADERO, CALIFORNIA 93423-6016
www.impactpublishers.com

Contents

Introduction *1*

CHAPTER 1: How Custody Decisions Are Made: An Overview 5

Young Children and Preteens 5
Mature Preteens and Teenagers: Voting With Their Feet 7
If Teenagers Vote With Their Feet, What Is the Voting Age? 9
How Do Children Make Their Wishes Known? 9
By What Process Does the Custody Evaluator
    Arrive at a Recommendation? 10
Who Is the Most Important Person to Persuade
    in a Court Custody Dispute? 12
Temporary Versus Permanent Custody 13
What You Can Do If the Other Parent Is Awarded
    Custody by an *Ex Parte* Order Without Notice to You? 15
Will the Judge Rubber-Stamp the Temporary Custody Award
    at the Time of the Decision on Permanent Custody? 16
What Should You Do If the Evaluator's Recommendation
    Goes Against You? 18
If You Decide to Contest the Recommendation of the
    Neutral Evaluator, How Should You Go About It? 19

Chapter 2: How to Conduct Yourself During the Custody Evaluation 23

The Initial Interview 24
Should You Go Negative in Your "Campaign" for Custody? 29
You and Your Child Meet Together With the Evaluator 30
Tell the Truth; Don't Exaggerate 32
Whose Child Is It? 33
Private Versus Public Evaluation 33
When Is a Private Evaluator to Be Preferred? 33

Chapter 3: The Role of Attorneys in Custody Litigation 39

Do You Need an Attorney to Represent You? 39
How to Choose an Attorney 42
How Will You Know If an Attorney Has Sufficient
    Experience to Handle Your Custody Case? 45
Whom Should You Not Hire? 46
How Do You Choose an Attorney to Represent You? 46
Changing Attorneys — Beware of the Stigma Involved 48
Suppose Your Attorney Wants to Withdraw from the Case? 50

Chapter 4: Protecting Your Child 53

Protecting Your Child Will Not Hurt Your Custody Case 53
How Do Most Parents Act? 55
The Symptoms of Emotional Damage 56
What Can Divorcing Parents Do to Protect Their Children? 57
What Kind of Therapist Do Children of Separation Need? 58
When Parents Are the Problem 69
Protecting Your Child From the Other Parent 61
Certain Persons Can Assist You in Proving
    Parental Alienation 62

Chapter 5: Possible Parenting Plans 67

Joint Custody/Equal Time-Sharing 68
The Standard Plan 69
Supervised Visitation 71
Suspended Visitation 71

Chapter 6: Psychological Evaluations 75

How to Approach a Psychological Evaluation 75
When Is a Complete Psychological Evaluation
    of the Parents Helpful? 76
What Are the Limitations of a Psychological Evaluation? 76
Who Gets Evaluated? 77
When Does the Evaluation Begin? 77
How Should You Act During a Psychological Evaluation? 78
What Psychological Testing Will Likely Be Required? 80
Can You "Beat" the Tests? 82
Confidentiality 82
What About Testing the Children? 84
Suppose a Psychological Evaluator Concludes
    That You Have a Personality Disorder? 85

Chapter 7: Relocation Cases: The Custodial
    Parent Can Move Away With the Children 89

A 180-Degree Change in the Law 89
...And Back Again — The Current Law 91
What If One Parent Under a Joint Custody Plan
    Wants to Relocate With the Children? 92
The Effect of *Burgess* on Child Custody Litigation 94
The Effect of *Burgess* on Other States 94
Do Not Relocate Your Children Without the Permission of
    a Court or the Written Permission of the Other Parent 95

Chapter 8: Child Abuse and False
    Accusations of Molestation 99

What Constitutes Neglect of a Child? 100
What If the Judge Concludes That a Child Is Being Abused? 101
The Molestation Charge 102
How to Respond to a Charge of Child Molestation 103

Chapter 9: Domestic Violence:
    Things Have Changed 109

How to Protect Yourself and Your Children 110
Should You Reveal Abuse to the Custody Evaluator? 112

Warn the Courthouse Deputies in Advance That a
   Dangerous Person Will Be Present at the Courthouse 113
What About Your Safety After a Court Hearing? 114
How the Law Treats the Custody Rights of Abusers 114

Chapter 10: Parental Alienation 117

Evidence of Parental Alienation 118
What Can Be Done About Parental Alienation? 119
Alienation During Abduction 121
Proving That the Other Parent Is Alienating the Child 122

Chapter 11: Will the Court Be Fair? Gender Bias, Forum Shopping, and Challenges 125

Bias on the Bench? 125
Should You Shop for a Judge? 127
Challenging a Judge — Peremptory 128
Challenging a Judge — Cause 129

Chapter 12: Child Support 133

Variations Among the States 134
Factors Determining Child Support 134
Parent Income and Child Support 135
New-Mate Income 136
High-Income Parents 137
Unemployed by Choice — "Really Lazy" Parents 138
Multiple Families — The Battle for Dollars 139
Parent Expenses and Child Support 141
Health Care and Medical Expenses 141
Child Care Expenses 141
Assigning Wages for Support 142
What Are We Fighting About? 142
The Attitude of Judges Toward Child Support Schedules 143

Chapter 13: Attorneys and Fees in Custody Litigation 147

How Much Will It Cost? 147
Do I Really Need an Attorney in a Custody Case? 148

Should You Be Your Own Attorney? 148
Will Fees Be Awarded to the Low Earner? 149

Glossary 153
Index 163

Foreword

The most important advice Judge James W. Stewart offers in this book is that *you are in charge of managing your child custody case.* This is not a do-it-yourself manual for those who want to do it without a lawyer. Judge Stewart offers thoughtful and practical advice for selecting a lawyer, and stern warnings against the folly of proceeding without one. But retaining a lawyer does not, and should not, mean that you are giving up control and management of your case. The best lawyers want their *clients* to make the important decisions, and want those decisions to be as well-informed as possible. Good lawyers will celebrate the availability of the advice Judge Stewart has for their clients. They should consider providing their clients with a copy of this book. (If you got this book from your lawyer, you know you're in good hands!)

In a dispute over child custody, you are being judged in every aspect at every moment. You are being judged by evaluators and therapists. You are being judged by your own attorney. You are being judged by opposing counsel. And, of course, you are being judged by the judge. With remarkable candor, Judge Stewart offers suggestions to present yourself and your case in the best light possible.

Traps and pitfalls abound in child custody disputes. Any litigation is a painful experience for a client to go through, but child custody litigation is certainly the most gut-wrenching experience of all. Clients going through this experience need clear and direct guidelines. The "Do's and Don'ts" which sum up each chapter of this book do tell it like it is, and don't mince words. They spell things out with clarity and authority.

Judge Stewart has seen all the mistakes and mishaps, and knows the pain and the costs they extract. Most of his twenty years on the bench has been in family law, where he chooses to serve. Many judges dread assignment to family court, and count the days to their reassignment elsewhere. Judge Stewart chooses to serve in family court because he truly wants to help families put their lives back together.

This is an honest and compelling book, packed with wisdom, from a man who has been there, day in and day out. His advice will save you money. More important, it will save you lots of headaches and heartaches.

Gerald F. Uelmen
Professor of Law
Santa Clara University School of Law
Santa Clara, California
February 1, 2000

Acknowledgements

My very special thanks to Laura Morgan, Senior Attorney at the National Legal Research Group of Charlottesville, Virginia, whose willingness to share with me her knowledge of the child support law of every state, and whose pro bono *research to meet the special needs of this book, have allowed me to write a chapter on child support that will be useful nationwide. Thanks also to Terry Johnston, Ph.D., who wrote the chapter on Psychological Evaluation in collaboration with me, and to my developmental editor/literary agent, Ward Winslow, for his untiring efforts to make this book more readable for the general public.*

Introduction

This book is intended to fully, clearly, and concisely explain to the reader the process of court child custody litigation. It will show you how custody decisions are made in our courts, what you can expect at each stage of the process, and things you can do to insure that your abilities as a parent are clearly presented to those persons with influence over the custody decision in your case. It is intended to eliminate surprises for you that could lead to costly mistakes along the way. This book, along with the advice and leadership of a capable and experienced attorney, will allow you to present your case for custody in its best possible light.

You should know, however, that no book, including this one, can alone bring you success in a custody dispute. Books entitled "How to Win..., etc." are fraudulent to the extent that they hold out the promise that there is some secret to prevailing in a custody dispute that will be revealed in the book. (I recently found one of these pieces of rubbish selling for $89 on the Internet.) Indeed, no single lawyer is a guarantor of success in a custody case. If you believe that the strategies and information from a book or from the "right" lawyer will by themselves bring you success in a custody dispute regardless of your ability to parent and nurture a child, you must set that notion aside immediately or it will adversely affect you and the outcome of your case.

A word about what this book is not intended to do. While it makes suggestions concerning how to best present your case to a custody evaluator and to the judge, it is not intended to suggest that you attempt to be someone or something you are not. In fact you cannot successfully do so. The facts upon which your case will be decided are in large measure already established. Your ability to parent a child is part of your personality structure, which was likely established years ago. However, in a very close case in which the parenting skills or lack thereof are almost equal, a capable attorney experienced in custody matters, as well as information available in this book, can affect the outcome. But books and attorneys are merely aids to you, not a guarantee of what you perceive to be a successful outcome.

You should also know that it is almost always in your children's best interest to settle a case either with or without mediation rather than to litigate in court. Most parents know immediately what parenting plan is in their children's best interests and they agree to that plan quickly or at least long before trial. These parents, rather than the state, are able to determine how their children will be raised. Their children will have certainty in their lives as to their future far sooner than children of parents in protracted custody litigation. They will have avoided the rancor and hostility of a custody trial that makes future cooperation in raising the children almost impossible. They are less likely to return to court over and over again because an agreement has been reached that both parents can live with.

Moreover, parents who settle custody disputes will not spend the funds that the children could well use later in life for a college education or as the down payment on a new home. In fact some parents spend so much in custody litigation that their own ability to ever own another home becomes doubtful. It is almost impossible to wage full-blown custody litigation for less than $50,000 per parent, assuming that both parents have attorneys. This judge has seen custody disputes where each side has spent well in excess of $150,000. Whatever the amount spent, it is normally a sufficient percentage of the parties' savings or future earnings that they and the children are later deprived of things they would like to be able to afford. Moreover, the expenditure of one's life savings on litigation is not gender-neutral. It is especially tragic for the traditional mother and homemaker. After many years of raising and nurturing children at home, she, unlike her husband, does not have the career, skills, or work experience that will lead to employment at a level that will generate the income required for home ownership.

Of course you cannot agree to a parenting plan that you and any competent expert in the needs and behavior of children believes will be detrimental or harmful to your children. But if you get to the trial stage of custody litigation, you will be in that 3 percent of all custody filings that judges see for an extended period. It is likely that the relationship between you and the other parent is totally dysfunctional, that at least one of you has serious emotional problems, and that one parent is using the litigation as a way to hurt the other parent, obtain personal vindication, or ventilate anger and rage at the failure of the marriage. These are what mental health professionals and judges refer to as "hidden agendas" in divorce cases. It is also likely that one of the parents has a serious personality disorder that is not readily subject to treatment. Such parents will not accept the recommendations of any number of mediators or evaluators, and indeed when the result of the case is adverse to their goals, will claim that the system, the evaluator, and the judge are flawed or biased against them or their gender. This book cannot influence these parents or help them. It will not assist them to conceal their hidden agendas or to conceal their inadequacies as a parent. If your spouse or the other parent is one of these disordered people, you are in for a very tough ride through the courts that can be minimized if you will listen to your attorney, and use the information available in this book.

1.

How Custody Decisions Are Made: An Overview

H ere's a fundamental fact about custody decisions: *If the parents cannot settle a custody arrangement, the court* — that is, the judge, with help from a custody evaluator — *will decide.* So you and your ex-spouse will make the most basic decision: to decide for yourselves, or to let the court decide for you. This chapter will examine how the court will proceed, if you allow it to do so.

Young Children and Preteens

In determining which parent should have primary custody of a young child or preteen, or whether a form of joint custody is the appropriate award, courts (judges and evaluators) are usually guided by the answers to the following five questions:

1. To which parent is the child or children more closely attached or bonded? To say that a child is attached or bonded to a parent is to say that the child is comfortable, secure, and relaxed with that parent and relies upon that parent to meet the majority of the child's needs. The parent to whom the child is more closely bonded is sometimes referred to as the "primary psychological parent" or the "primary nurturing parent." The latter refers to the parent who has taken the greatest responsibility for the child, providing transportation, preparing food, helping with schoolwork, and putting the child to bed at night. While this parent is not necessarily the parent to whom the child is more closely attached, there is a high correlation between the two roles.

2. *Which parent has the greater ability to provide structure, consistency, and limits in a child's life?* To provide *structure* is to say that roles and authority and expectations within the family are clearly defined and understood. To provide *consistency* is to provide routine in a child's life with which the child is comfortable and can rely on. Children with consistency in their lives know what can be expected of them each day, and are sure of being treated in a consistent manner by the parent. To set *limits* is to make it clear to a child in an appropriate manner what behavior is or is not acceptable: proper behavior is rewarded; unacceptable conduct is brought to a halt and, if necessary, punished in a proper and loving way (e.g., the child should never doubt the parent's love, or be made to feel like a bad or "flawed" person).

It is important to remember that the needs of children change as they grow older. Comfort and security are the most important factors in the life of an infant, toddler, and preschooler. As the child grows older, the need for structure and consistency increases. A teenager needs limits, routines, and responsibilities very different from those appropriate to a 3-year-old. Flexibility is an important parent quality.

3. *Which parent will more strongly support the child's relationship with the other parent?* In some states, statutes require that this factor be considered in the process of arriving at the best parenting plan for the child. While probably not as important as factors 1 and 2, this item can tip the scales in some cases, and the parent who is most able to share the child with the other parent will likely get the nod. Recent studies have established that high conflict between separating parents has long-term harmful effects on a child's emotional well-being.

4. *Who can better assist the child to achieve success in school so as to give the child more choices in life?* This goes beyond the question of who helps the child with homework, and includes the parent's ability to communicate the importance of education, learning, and academic success. As children start school, the need for nurturing and comfort recedes and the need for achievement

increases. If a child has not achieved some degree of success in schoolwork by the third or fourth grade, the child's self-esteem and confidence will be eroded, the child may cease to try to do well in school, and may look for friends among other children who have been unsuccessful.

5. *Which parent is more likely to give the child freedom to grow into a capable and self-sufficient adult?* This factor, of course, grows more important as the child grows older and reaches the preteen years. Some parents are overly enmeshed or invested in their children. They want to be in control of every moment of a child's life and are anxious and insecure if the child is away from them even to be in school or to play or socialize with friends. They may try to discourage peer relationships, educate the child at home, and/or make other efforts to guard against outside influences, fearing loss of control over the child or competition with the parent-child relationship. They are almost always hostile to access to the child by the other parent because it might weaken the child's loyalty to them. These parents are often very needy, and arrange family life so that their children meet their needs as much as, or more than, they meet the children's needs. Children of such parents are in danger of growing up in a role-reversal situation that will limit their ability to relate properly with others. These children often try to protect, nurture, and take responsibility for the needy parent out of a fear of losing that parent. Psychologists often refer to these children as "parentified."

In summary then, your chances of being awarded the primary custody of your child are enhanced if you have spent more time caring for your child than has the other parent, if you have put a young child to bed at night with a story and a hug, if you have helped the child with schoolwork and taken part in school activities, if your conduct reflects a belief that the child needs two parents, if you provide structure and consistency in your child's life, and if you demonstrate your ability to give your child room to breathe and grow.

Mature Preteens and Teenagers: Voting With Their Feet

We often say that "teenagers vote with their feet." By this we mean that judges are very reluctant to place a teenage child in a custody relationship that is contrary to the expressed wishes of the teenager. They fear that the teenager may simply refuse to obey the court order and will run away, or that such a placement will result in a hostile, rebellious, and obstreperous child the custodial parent cannot control. This is true even if the judge believes that the desires of the child are the result of a calculated campaign by one parent to alienate the child from the other parent. When a child is age 6 the judge can make a custody placement for the purpose of ending or reversing a campaign of alienation that emotionally damages the child. At age 15, it is too late. It may well be too late at age 8.

There are a few situations in which a judge will not follow the expressed wishes of the teenager or mature preteen. This can occur if the child is failing in school and the judge senses that the child's parent of choice is unable to provide the structure, consistency, and limits necessary for success in school. In addition, if the teenager appears to be motivated solely by a desire to live with a permissive parent so as to avoid reasonable parental authority, the judge may decline to follow the child's wishes and simply say to the child that "if you run away, then you will go to the children's shelter or a group home placement until you agree not to do so."

I recall a case over which I presided several years ago in which the father invited his daughter's boyfriend to spend the night with his daughter when she was in his custody. Moreover, when he called the teenager at her mother's home, he would arrange to put the boyfriend on the phone to encourage the daughter to return to the father's home so that she could be with the boyfriend. In an earlier placement with the father, the girl was failing in school, but in the custody of the mother, the child's grades were quite acceptable. No reasonable person would have recommended that the teenager's preference to live with the father be honored.

Finally, there are the teenagers who are simply manipulating their parents and the court system to get their way. Whenever one parent seeks to impose limits or exert reasonable authority, these teenagers respond by saying that they want to live with the other parent. They express a different preference to the court every few months. The only way the judge can bring an end to the game is to place the teenager with the parent most able to provide and enforce structure and limits, and to let the teenager know that the only option is the children's shelter or a group home placement.

If Teenagers Vote with Their Feet, What Is the Voting Age?

At what age will the child's preferences be the most important factor in determining which parent should be awarded primary custody? Eight? Ten? Fourteen?

Judges will "consider" the preferences of a child of any age sufficient to express a preference. However, a child's preference is not apt to be the determining factor in a custody award until the child is about 12. Obviously the very mature and thoughtful 10-year-old and the immature and rebellious 13-year-old would be exceptions to the rule.

The older a child is, even if under 12, the more weight a judge will give to the child's preferences. However, most children under about 12 are easily manipulated and open to suggestion by their parents. More importantly, children under that age generally want to stay out of the line of fire in a dispute that is so bitter that it has reached the trial stage. Younger children normally don't want to disappoint either parent and every ounce of their emotional energy is spent trying to appease both parents. (This is one reason for the common fall in school grades at the time of separation.) Indeed, children will privately tell each parent what that parent wants to hear. The last thing the child wants to do is express a preference for one parent over the other, even though the child may secretly hold a preference.

As children reach the teen years, while still subject to some manipulation, they are not as reluctant to express a preference. Unfortunately, teens often express not only a preference, but may take the side of one parent in the divorce and become estranged from the other parent. Indeed, being judgmental and taking sides may be what teenagers do best! This estrangement from one parent does not portend well for their emotional health as they grow into adulthood.

How Do Children Make Their Wishes Known?

It is a rare child whose preferences are expressed as a witness in open court. Few judges will tolerate placing children in this position, considering it to be almost an act of child abuse. Young children are intimidated by the experience of testifying and feel that they have been stripped of their privacy. Teenagers who want to testify so that they can "take sides" publicly should not be given the sense of power and control over the parents that would come with such open-court testimony.

The appropriate venue for children to express their views is to the evaluator. The preference can be received as evidence of the child's state of mind when the evaluator makes a report and testifies in court. Young children should be assured that the decision is not theirs to make. The decision is the judge's and they will not be blamed.

Some judges will meet with children privately in chambers in order to determine their wishes. Other judges feel — and I agree — that the trained mental health professional is better qualified to receive the opinion without doing damage to the child.

If an attorney has been appointed to represent a child, the attorney is obligated to convey the client's wishes to the court, although most courts will want children's attorneys to express their own opinions of what parenting plan is best for the child, even though the attorney's view may be different than the child's. Courts will permit this divergence from the position of the child because the attorney is seen as a form of guardian who represents the child's best interest as well as the child.

By What Process Does the Custody Evaluator Arrive at a Recommendation?

The evaluator will certainly interview both parents as sources of information. The interview may be with the parents together, with each separately, or both. If the children are above the age of 5, the evaluator may wish to interview them in an effort to determine which parent provides a sense of well-being and security.

A competent evaluator will never ask a preteen child the ultimate question: "With which parent do you want to live?" Rather, the evaluator may ask the child what she enjoys most at each parent's home, what three or four things he likes most and least about each parent, to which parent does she take personal problems, and/or which parent helps with homework and talks to teachers. Questions such as these will normally reveal the child's comfort level with each parent. At times, the level may be about equal.

Good evaluators learn the most about the relationship between a young child and a parent by watching the parent and child interact together. This will reveal how relaxed the child is with the parent, and how loving the child is toward that parent. Of course, watching a child interact with a parent will also show whether the child is fearful or intimidated by the parent. Perhaps of equal importance, the evaluator can see whether a parent knows how to properly relate with, play with, and set limits for a child. The evaluator may observe from the same room, or from another room through a one-way mirror so that the evaluator's presence will not distract the child. You should be aware that at times the evaluator can learn a great deal by simply watching a child with one or both parents as they sit in the waiting room waiting to be interviewed. Of course at that point the parents would not know that they were being observed.

In the following chapter we will discuss custody evaluations in detail and how you should conduct yourself during an evaluation interview — both with and without your child — in order that your strengths as a parent will be properly conveyed.

Sometimes an evaluator will want psychological evaluations of the parents, perhaps including psychological testing. Such an evaluation is done in only a small number of cases, since the average custody case is not so difficult that psychological evaluations and testing are required. However, in very complex and complicated cases where one or both parents may appear to have a hidden agenda, psychological evaluations are helpful. Here are a few examples: One parent is charged with alienating or attempting to bias the children against the other parent; one parent appears unable to follow a court-ordered custody and visitation plan; one parent or a new mate is charged by the other parent with having abused or molested a child and the charge is vehemently denied.

How you should conduct yourself at a psychological evaluation will be discussed in chapter 6.

The evaluator may also want to talk with day-care providers, teachers, and certainly the child's attorney and therapist if the child has either one. An evaluator will seldom talk to everyone a parent wishes the evaluator to interview. Many parents come to an evaluation with a laundry list of witness-allies who will attest to that parent's abilities to care for children. When the evaluator declines to interview the entire list, the parent may feel that the evaluator did not do a thorough job. However, many witnesses — such as relatives or close friends of a parent — are not seen as likely to have an objective view of the situation. If the evaluator is a county or court employee, that person's workload is overwhelming and time is not available to do interviews solely to satisfy one parent. Private evaluators may have more time, but they are hesitant to charge the parties for interviews that are almost certain not to be helpful. Most evaluators will conduct interviews until they believe they have a firm grasp on the dynamics of the relationship between the parents and what parenting plan is in the child's best interest. Interviews will cease when the interviewer is confident that his or her opinion has sufficient support to stand up under cross-examination, including questions about the persons who were not interviewed.

Experienced evaluators and attorneys know that it is seldom effective cross-examination to ask the evaluator why he or she did not interview this or that neighbor, or friend, or relative if the evaluator has spent sufficient time with the parents and those persons who can truly be helpful in giving the evaluator insight into a child's needs and the parent's abilities as care givers.

Who is the Most Important Person to Persuade in a Court Custody Dispute?

It is not the judge. The judge will make the ultimate decision, of course, but the recommendation of a court-appointed neutral evaluator is adopted by the judge without substantial change in the vast majority of cases — perhaps as high as 85 percent. For a parent to believe that he or she can prevail in a custody dispute by a direct appeal to the judge — ignoring the evaluator's recom- mendation — would be a costly miscalculation of how the system works. Thus, since the neutral evaluator's opinion is often pivotal, your attorney needs to know as much, if not more, about the preferences, tendencies, and biases of any person who might be appointed by the court to evaluate your case as your attorney should know about any judge to whom your case might be assigned. This fact alone explains why you should be represented by a local attorney who has extensive custody-case experience in the jurisdic- tion where your case will be heard. The selection of an attorney will be discussed at length in chapter 3.

An excellent study of the outcomes of custody cases in a major metropolitan court revealed that the two factors that most influence a judge's custody decision were the recommendations of the evaluator and the preferences of the child. While the results of the study did not reveal the age of each child interviewed, it is likely that the recommendation of the evaluator was the most important factor in cases involving custody of young children, and the preference of the child was given greater weight in cases involving older children. It is also likely that when both factors favored the same parent, that parent was awarded custody in virtually all such cases.

You should keep in mind that the evaluators referred to in this chapter are *neutral* evaluators appointed by the judge or agreed upon by the parties and then appointed by the judge. Experts retained and paid by only one party do not normally have nearly as much influence with the judge as the independent evaluator appointed by the judge. Judges with experience know that in any area of law, privately retained forensic experts — referred to pejoratively as "hired guns" — tend to tilt their opinions in favor of the party who has hired and paid them. When they testify they do not usually take the witness stand with as high a level of credibility as the truly independent evaluator. That is not to say that the testimony of an expert allied with one side will never overcome the testimony of the independent expert appointed by the court.

Temporary Versus Permanent Custody

A "temporary" custody award is an award made prior to the completion of an evaluation of a child's best interests and a hearing or trial on that evaluation, if necessary. The award of temporary custody may be made after a brief hearing, but it may also be made *"ex parte"* — without a hearing before a judicial officer. Indeed, while normally effective for only a short period of time, an *ex parte* order can be made in favor of one parent before the other parent is even aware that a divorce or paternity action has been filed with the court. That's because the other parent may be served with papers that commence the litigation after the *ex parte* custody order has been signed by the judge.

In order to obtain an *ex parte* order, one parent may place before a judge a written affidavit or declaration that a temporary custody award is required pending a hearing because the child will be subject to some risk or danger if the award is not made. In the affidavit or declaration, one parent may swear under oath that the other parent may neglect or abuse the child, or flee the jurisdiction with the child if an *ex parte* order is not made pending a later hearing. These are but a few of the imminent dangers that are often alleged in order to obtain *ex parte* custody awards. These allegations often involve conduct while under the influence of drugs or alcohol. An *ex parte* order lasts only until a hearing is held. That hearing will usually be for the purpose of setting a further temporary custody order (pending evaluation and trial); the date for the hearing is usually set by the judge in the papers granting the *ex parte* custody award.

Please note that "*ex parte*" means without a hearing. It does not mean without notice. An *ex parte* award can be made either with or without notice to the other side, although the urgency of the situation alleged in the affidavit often results in the other parent not having notice that the *ex parte* order is being sought. When notice is given, the other parent is normally given an opportunity to submit a counterdeclaration or appear in court before the judge signs or denies the *ex parte* order.

In order to reduce the possibility that an *ex parte* order of custody will be made in favor of the other parent without notice to you, as soon as you have retained an attorney, have your attorney notify both the other parent's attorney as well as any judge likely to receive an *ex parte* request that your attorney wishes to have time to respond to any *ex parte* request for custody. If you have not yet retained an attorney, then give notice that you want notice sent to you. The request is more likely to be honored if you have an attorney, because neither the judge nor the other parent's attorney will want to offend an attorney with whom they may have many future cases.

At the hearing (several weeks later), both parties will have an opportunity to be heard in testimony before the court. The hearing may be before the judge only, or it may involve a "mini" evaluation by a court-appointed expert, usually a court or county employee. That person will be asked to evaluate the charges one parent has made against the other and to recommend a parenting plan that will remain in place until a full evaluation can be completed. The evaluator will normally have a recommendation the same day if not within an hour or two. The evaluator is not attempting to determine the long-range best interests of the children, but merely to find a parenting plan under which they will be safe from harm and allow both parents as much access as is consistent with their welfare and safety.

What Can You Do If the Other Parent Is Awarded Custody by an *Ex parte* Order Without Notice to You?

There is nothing you can do if the affidavit or declaration on which the judge based the award is factually correct. However, the affidavit may be a mixture of outright misrepresentations, half-truths, and omissions — not at all rare in custody disputes. One alternative is to do nothing until the hearing a few weeks later and then put the true facts before the judge or evaluator assigned to do an emergency or "mini" assessment. This is often the best course so long as the *ex parte* order itself does not put your child in harm's way. That choice also saves money. Your only other recourse is to put before the judge your own affidavit and that of some independent witnesses in conjunction with a request that the judge vacate the *ex parte* custody order. But it is extremely difficult to prove the falsity of allegations and charges against you simply by denying them in writing. However, if you believe that you can prove the other parent's allegations to be false and you fear that the *ex parte* order will harm your children, then you should act. Indeed a failure to do so may subject you to later criticism. For example, assume the parent granted an *ex parte* award of custody has omitted a history of drug, alcohol, spousal, or child abuse from the declaration and you have access to court or police records that will establish the history. When you attach them to your own affidavit asking the judge to set aside the *ex parte* order, they will carry great weight. However, at this point you or your attorney knows the address of the other parent or the identity of the other parent's attorney, so you should give notice that you are seeking a reversal of the *ex parte* custody award by sending the attorney a copy of your affidavit before it is presented to the judge. When your request is presented with your affidavit, the judge has three options. The judge can take no action if she believes that the child is not at risk pending the hearing. The judge can reverse the original order and make an *ex parte* custody award to you. That is unlikely unless your declaration is so compelling that the judge believes that the other parent has deceived the court. The more likely course is that the judge, uncertain of where the truth lies, will order everyone to the courthouse for a short hearing perhaps in conjunction with a "mini" assessment, wherein a trained mental health professional can spend an hour or so getting to the truth of the matter.

(The judge is never likely simply to vacate the original award of custody and leave the parents without an order pending the hearing. The judge is quite aware that such a course can lead to day-to-day confrontations at best and physical force or violence at worst.)

It would be surprising if you incurred less than $3,500 in attorney fees trying to reverse the *ex parte* order. Of course, if you are successful in reversing the *ex parte* order either by affidavit or at the scheduled hearing, you can certainly ask that the parent whose affidavit proved untrustworthy pay the attorney fees you incurred in putting the true facts before the court. The law of almost every state will permit an award of fees where one parent has deceived the court and has cost the other parent substantial fees in establishing the truth. It should also be noted that at this point the file is forever tainted against the parent who deceived the court and, to a lesser extent, against the attorney representing that parent. All future evidence presented by that parent at the permanent custody hearing will be received with skepticism by the evaluator and the judge. Thus it is almost always counterproductive to submit a misleading affidavit in order to obtain an *ex parte* award of custody. As a result of such an action, you may receive less access to your child than you would have been awarded had you admitted facts that were unflattering to you.

Will the Judge Rubber-Stamp the Temporary Custody Award at the Time of the Decision on Permanent Custody?

At the hearing on the *ex parte* order, an award of temporary custody will be made. The order will remain in effect until the evaluation of permanent custody is complete and a hearing on the evaluation can be held, if required.

Assume the temporary custody order goes against you. Will the judge at the time of the hearing on permanent custody simply rubber-stamp the temporary award and make it the permanent award? In theory this is not ever supposed to happen. In every state a permanent custody evaluation and hearing is supposed to be a fresh look at the long-term best interests of the child(ren), without regard to the temporary or interim custody award. The temporary award was merely to find an interim plan that will assure a child's safety and welfare pending an evaluation. It often involves nothing more than keeping in place a status quo that existed before the case came to court. It would violate the law to allow the temporary award to create a status quo that is rubber-stamped at the time of the hearing on permanent custody.

Unfortunately, experienced family law attorneys hold the strong belief that judges and evaluators who hear cases at the permanent custody stage start with a strong presumption that the status quo created by the temporary award should be the permanent award. One can only conclude that there must be some truth to the charge, since its validity is so universally accepted. It does not, however, comport with my experience as a Family Court judge, seeing only the cases that do not settle prior to a trial on permanent custody. Cases in which the recommendation reverses or radically changes the temporary award may be more apt to go to hearing; the temporary custodian of the children likely sees the temporary award as a status quo to be maintained and is unlikely to accept a major modification of the temporary award without demanding a trial before a judge. Perhaps there is some large number of cases I do not see where the recommendation of the evaluator is to maintain the status quo and the dissatisfied parent, having adjusted to the temporary plan, does not wish to spend the money and emotional energy needed to bring the case to a trial.

Since most judges hold the view that the temporary award should not be presumed to be in the children's long-term best interests, there is something you or your attorney can do if the temporary award is adverse to you and you are concerned that it will later be presumed to be the proper permanent custody award. Ask the judge to write into the temporary custody order before it is signed: "This temporary award of custody shall not establish a status quo for purposes of determining a permanent custody plan." The only possible reason the judge could give for refusing to do so is that the statement merely states the law and thus there is no purpose is writing it into the order. At that point your attorney might suggest that it is possible the permanent custody hearing will be held before a judge less experienced in family law. In any event, the written statement will serve as a reminder to the permanent custody evaluator that the temporary order creates no presumption as to what the permanent custody award should be. Some judges may prefer the statement that, "This order is without prejudice to either party." It means the same thing.

What Should You Do If the Evaluator's Recommendation Goes Against You?

You will have the recommendations of the evaluator for some period of time before your case goes to trial on the issue of permanent custody. Most states require by statute that you have the recommendation a minimum number of days before the trial. Once that recommendation is made, the case may well be over. As stated earlier, the neutral evaluator's recommendation is followed in the vast majority of cases. (A recent study at the University of California at San Diego confirms this fact.) You are at a crossroads in the case and you must determine whether to continue the litigation on to a trial despite the fact that the odds are now weighted heavily against you.

However, in addition to that fact, you should consider several other things. What will be the affect on the children of continued litigation that leaves them in doubt about their future for a longer period of time and subjects them to still another intrusive interview or observation by a stranger? What is the reputation of your evaluator with the judges of the court for making correct recommendations in custody cases that are generally followed? Will the errors or false assumptions that you find in the evaluator's report be apparent to the judge? Can you afford the additional $15,000 to $40,000 in attorney and expert fees that a custody trial will cost you?

At this point, you need the advice of your attorney. If you have chosen an experienced and capable family law attorney with the integrity to be candid with you, you are indeed fortunate. You can receive invaluable advice from someone familiar with your judge and your evaluator. If you are uncertain of your attorney's judgment or insight in the matter, by all means take the report and recommendation to another attorney for a second opinion. However, you should make it clear to that attorney that you will not retain her to represent you at a trial. In that way you will insure an objective second opinion by removing any possibility that the attorney rendering the "second opinion" will be motivated to advise continued litigation by the desire to earn a substantial fee.

If You Decide to Contest the Recommendation of the Neutral Evaluator, How Should You Go About It?

If you do decide to go to trial on the issue of custody, there is one traditional approach that is almost worthless. Under this scenario your attorney picks up the telephone and retains a well-known forensic psychologist who is known to be willing to do an evaluation and give testimony on behalf of whichever parent "hires" him in custody litigation and has the reputation of being "helpful" to that parent. If your attorney is aware of that individual's reputation, it is very likely that the judge is also aware or will become aware during the course of the trial. This expert will have a most difficult time establishing credibility with the judge. It will be virtually impossible unless the expert has interviewed both parents and interviewed or observed the children (except for very young children), spoken with other witnesses, and seen all documents that the judge would consider necessary to an informed opinion. The only expert who should be even remotely considered for the task of judging the validity of the recommendation of the court's appointed expert is a mental health professional with impeccable credentials for objectivity, who is often appointed as the court's expert, who seldom accepts employment by one parent only, and, if possible, is regularly invited by local judges to sit with them on panels is which child custody issues are addressed. Such an expert is extremely hard to find.

Unfortunately, the reality of your situation is that if you do not have an expert to challenge the opinion of the court-appointed evaluator, it is virtually impossible for you to prevail. Custody cases are seldom won because of the compelling personal characteristics of a parent or the brilliant cross-examination of that parent's attorney that shatters the opinions and conclusions of the court-appointed independent expert. That makes for good television drama, but seldom happens in real life.

There is another possible approach for someone in your dilemma that I strongly recommend: Have your attorney ask the judge to appoint a second expert as the court's own witness for the purpose of rendering a second opinion. In that way this second expert will have the same credibility with the judge as the expert appointed initially. Your attorney should assure the judge that you are willing to pay for the second opinion, and, if the recommendation of the second expert is substantially the same as that of the court's initial expert, then you are prepared to settle the matter on the terms of those recommendations. The expert appointed to render the second opinion will be told that it is a second opinion but will not be permitted to see the report of the initial evaluator or know the identity of that person. Your attorney can point out to the judge that, if the two experts have the same opinion, the court will avoid a trial that will escalate bitterness and lead to even further litigation. On the other hand, if the second opinion is at odds with the initial evaluation, the court will learn that this is a very close and difficult case that is deserving of a trial. If your judge sees a trial as more harmful to the children than an interview by another mental health professional, your request may indeed be granted. In order to receive such a ruling, your attorney may also need to persuade the judge that such a second opinion could be completed by the time that said attorney would need to prepare for trial.

DO'S AND DON'TS

Do . . .

• Always keep in mind that a neutral custody evaluator rather than the judge will be the person who will have the greatest impact on the outcome of your case.

• Be aware that the judge may make an award of temporary custody without a hearing. Try to determine the identity of the other parent's attorney and give notice to the attorney and the judge that you want a chance to respond to any request for a custody order without a hearing.

• Note that in some jurisdictions a temporary custody award may be presumed to be the award that is in the children's long-term best interests at the hearing on permanent custody. If a temporary custody award is adverse to you, ask the judge to state in the order that the temporary award will not create a status quo or is without prejudice.

• Be aware that the evaluator may be assessing your relationship with your child as you sit in the waiting room prior to an appointment.

Don't . . .

• Don't ever call a child subject to a custody dispute as a witness in the case. You will probably antagonize the judge, and your judgment about what is good for children will be brought into question. Rather, request that the child be interviewed by the evaluator or privately in chambers by the judge.

• Don't assume that a custody evaluator retained and paid by you to testify for your side of the case will have the same standing with the judge as the neutral evaluator the judge has appointed. If the recommendation of the neutral evaluator goes against you, consider asking the judge to appoint another neutral evaluator to give a second opinion.

• Don't fail to reveal all facts about yourself and your relationship with the child in any request you make for an *ex parte* order for an award of custody. If you omit significant facts adverse to you, the award you receive may be overturned and your credibility will be forever tainted in the eyes of the judge.

• Don't believe that a failure by an evaluator to interview every person you offer to support your case will cause the judge to believe that the evaluation was not sufficiently thorough to support the recommendation.

2.

How to Conduct Yourself During the Custody Evaluation

I n this chapter we deal with your meetings with the *custody evaluator*. It's important to understand that a custody evaluator is not a *mediator*. A mediator simply attempts to get the parties to agree on a parenting plan. There are no consequences for either party if they do not agree. In many jurisdictions, what is said in mediation is confidential and cannot be brought before the judge. This is real *mediation*, as the term has traditionally been used. However, some state laws or local rules permit a mediator to recommend a parenting plan to the judge if an agreement is not reached. Under that procedure, your mediator is actually an *evaluator*. This arrangement is sometimes called "muscle mediation." ("Either you agree to this or I will take the matter to the judge who always follows my recommendations.")

You must know whether you are in real mediation or whether what you say may be repeated to the judge as part of a custody recommendation. Whether or not you are in real mediation as opposed to muscle mediation will affect both what you should say and what you may agree to. Discuss with your attorney — well in advance of any mediation date — the exact nature of any mediation in which you are ordered or volunteer to participate.

Keep in mind that we're discussing *evaluation*, not mediation or "muscle" mediation. A custody evaluation is similar to arbitration except that an arbitrator renders a decision and a custody evaluator makes a recommendation. The evaluation we deal with in this chapter is not a psychological evaluation, although the custody evaluator will certainly be interested in the emotional stability of both parents. The custody evaluator is the person with the duty to recommend to the judge a parenting plan that is in your children's best interests. Thus it is the evaluator who will have the greatest impact on the outcome of your case. Judges know that they are not trained in the needs or behavior of children at various stages of development. They know that they need guidance from someone with such training. If the recommendation appears to be based on sufficient and accurate information and flows logically from the evaluator's description of the parents and the children, the judge, as we've discussed, is highly likely to follow the recommendation.

The Initial Interview

If the judge or court personnel instruct you to make an appointment with an evaluator, do so promptly (within 48 hours). In all meetings with the evaluator, you should make every effort to be on time. You should never cancel an appointment unless the emergency is such that any reasonable person would expect you to do so. Above all, never fail to appear for an appointment without canceling. Punctuality tells the evaluator that you recognize the importance of the meeting to your children's future well-being. It shows that the needs of others are important to you, and that you do not have an overblown sense of your own importance, or a self-centered attitude that things will be done for your convenience. Punctuality gives the appearance of someone whose life is well-organized and who is capable of providing children with consistency and structure. The past experience of your evaluator is that parents who are tardy or cancel repeatedly or fail to appear for appointments tend to have emotional, drug, or alcohol problems. Thus when you do any of these things the evaluator will at least log the fact in the back of her mind and wonder about the significance.

Dress appropriately. Show by your dress that you know that you are in a very important meeting about your children's future. A skirt that is too tight, a blouse that is too skimpy, or makeup that is excessive may suggest that this mother's first priority is being attractive to men by superficial and suggestive means rather than caring for her children. Certain hairdos can suggest that you are overly concerned with physical appearance. A father in a tank-top shirt, or shorts, or sandals appears incapable of knowing what is appropriate for such a meeting. A father without a sense of propriety may be unable to provide a child with structure and limits.

I find it noteworthy that the study of evaluation outcomes at the University of California at San Diego — referred to in Chapter 1 — found that mothers described as "good" in physical appearance were more likely to be granted primary custody of the children. Do not confuse "good physical appearance" with physical attractiveness. It means well-groomed.

A colleague of mine with a wonderful sense of humor represented parents in a substantial number of custody cases in her law practice before she became a judicial officer. Early in her practice she told her female clients to "dress like a mother" in their meetings with the evaluator. When that did not appear to be a strong enough admonition, she told them to "dress like the judge's mother would dress." Finally she advised her clients to "dress as you think the judge would want her mother to dress."

It is vitally important that you appear focused. Answer the question thoughtfully and as succinctly as possible without omitting important information. The parent who does not answer the specific question asked, or who rambles along jumping from tangent to tangent, covering topics not necessary to answering the question asked, comes across as disorganized at best or having a rather flawed thought process at worst. Whichever conclusion the evaluator draws, you will not be seen as a reliable person who can provide a child with consistency, structure, and limits.

It is also important to make every effort not to cry. Obviously it is appropriate for an abused spouse to be emotional and even teary when describing the abuse. It may even be appropriate to be emotional when one still loves the other parent and is describing how that other parent was attracted to someone else. However, parents who are compelled to cry through a description of how the parties met, a description of the problems that led to the separation, a narration of how that parent meets the children's needs, or when asked to explain an allegation of alcohol or drug abuse, hurt their chances for an award of custody. Evaluators and judges find by experience that tears are seldom shed out of real concern for the plight of the children, but rather because the parent fears the personal embarrassment of an adverse custody award or is embarrassed by past questionable conduct. Indeed, parents who are not able to avoid a constant flow of tears will often appear "needy" to the evaluator. To say that a parent is needy is to say that the parent needs the relationship with the child more than the child is in need of the parent.

In addition to being asked to provide a history of your relationship with the other parent, you may be asked to describe your role, if any, as a caretaker of the child when you and the other parent resided together. You should give some thought to your answer before you go to the interview, and be able to say specifically how you contributed to caring for the children. The evaluator will be interested to know:

1. How often you helped the child get ready for school.
2. How often you prepared meals for the child.
3. How often you put the child to bed at night and read or told the child a short story.
4. The extent to which you provided the child with transportation to activities, to school, or to the doctor.
5. The extent to which you participated in child-centered activities such as playing in the park, playing games with the child, or attending athletic events, recitals, or birthday parties.
6. The degree to which you have been involved with your child's education by helping with homework, attending parent-teacher conferences, or volunteering at the school.
7. The extent to which you disciplined the child and the manner in which you did so when you found it necessary. The evaluator may wish to know the type of behavior that you believed called for discipline. You should be aware that evaluators are mental health professionals and the vast majority of them do not believe that corporal punishment (spanking, striking) is necessary or appropriate in the disciplining of a child. Indeed, many consider it child abuse.

As you describe your role as a caretaker, do not exaggerate. If the children do not corroborate your claims, either by way of what they say or how they relate to you, or if your claims are not consistent with the time you appeared to have had available, your credibility with the evaluator will be diminished. If you were not the primary nurturing parent, say so candidly and describe what you did contribute to caretaking. In many families, one parent, usually but not always the father, has the role of breadwinner and the other parent is the primary caretaker. This is nothing to be ashamed of. It is a reasonable division of labor for many parents. Moreover, the children may be very closely bonded to a parent who was not the primary caretaker and their best interests may require substantial and frequent access to that parent.

You should be prepared to state what you believe to be your strengths as a parent. If you admit to a deficiency or two it will not likely hurt your case, and you may well appear more credible as well as more perceptive as a result. Few parents excel in every role they must play as a parent. If the other parent has certain strengths, candidly say so. If you paint the other parent as a poor caretaker or a bad influence on the children, and neither the children nor anyone else corroborates your view, your insight, your motives, and your credibility are brought into question.

Strengths of good parenting would include being patient, being a good listener, and being calm in dealing with the children. A good parent is able to set and enforce limits in an effective but non-threatening manner. A willingness to devote sufficient time to the needs of your children is an important attribute of good parenting but very difficult to achieve if the parent has extensive work responsibilities. Children reflect a parent's good work in raising them by being comfortable in the parent's presence, by obeying the parent, and by confiding in the parent.

The evaluator may also want to know what temporary parenting plan is in place pending completion of the evaluation, and how it evolved. Was it agreed upon and why? Was it court-ordered? Was it simply the result of the force of greater physical strength by one party? The evaluator may also want your take on how the children have fared under the temporary plan.

If you have been the victim of abuse, you should candidly reveal that fact to the evaluator. It may affect the way the evaluation is structured (the parents may always be seen separately), as well as the components of the evaluation. (For example, psychological testing may be added.) If the children have witnessed the abuse, it is extremely important to let the evaluator know that fact. It may explain both your reactions as well as the children's to the abusive parent. The evaluator may want to have the mental health of the children evaluated or may want to recommend that they be placed in counseling with a licensed therapist. You must never hide the fact of abuse because you are embarrassed. Mental health professionals recognize that physical abuse is never the fault of the abused parent and that there is never any justification for it.

You may also be asked to suggest a parenting plan that will best meet your children's needs. If you are asked why you believe that you should be the primary custodial parent, frame your answers, if possible, in terms of the children's best interests. That demonstrates to the evaluator that you can keep your needs separate from the needs of the children, a task that many divorcing parents find quite daunting. For example, you might say, "Since I have been the primary caretaker during the marriage, the children are more comfortable with me and know that they can rely on me to meet their daily needs. I see it as in their best interests, during this time of turmoil in their lives, to have the continuity and assurance of living with the person who has always met their needs. It will allay their anxieties and fears to be able to live with someone they know they can rely on." Or, as another example, you might say, "It is probably also in the children's best interests to spend their weeks with me during the school year because I have been the one to monitor and help them with their homework and I have established relationships with their teachers."

If you disagree with a proposal made by the other parent or even by the evaluator, you should try to state your views in terms of the children's best interests. For example, the evaluator may suggest that the children reside with you during the week and with the other parent every weekend. You might very well ask, "Since I work during the week, is it really in the children's best interest not to have any leisure time at all with their primary custodial parent? We do a number of things on the weekend such as going to the beach, shopping for clothes, visiting with my parents, etc. ..." This sounds so much better than the response the evaluator is so used to hearing: "But that's not fair to me." It is not *your* best interests that the evaluator and the judge are interested in. The law mandates them to focus on the *children's* best interests.

Should You Go Negative in Your "Campaign" for Custody?

If you believe that the other parent has some glaring deficiencies in parenting ability, it is perfectly proper to point these out to the evaluator. Indeed if the deficiencies are such that would put your children at risk, you absolutely must point them out. However, don't let your interview turn into a litany of complaints against the other parent, and be especially careful to avoid talking so much about the other parent that you don't have time for a discussion of your strengths as a parent and your relationship to the children. Further, the way you state criticism is important. Try to state things in terms of what concerns you. Rather than saying, "I don't like the way he loses his temper and yells at the children and me," say, "It concerns me that the children seem so intimidated and fearful of their father because of the way he yells at all of us when he loses his temper." Or, "I am concerned that our son is starting to show the same kind of volatility and anger as his father. I just don't think that it is in his best interests to learn to control others by intimidation." Instead of saying, "She is always late to pick up the children for visitation and sometimes she never shows up at all," try a less frontal attack such as, "It concerns me to see the children so disappointed and hurt when Martha is late in picking them up or when she never shows up at all. I am afraid it will diminish their ability to trust others, and I don't think that is in their best interests as they grow into adults." Rather than saying, "Martha is dragging the kids into this litigation by talking to them constantly about custody issues," you might say, "It concerns me that if Martha continues to talk to the children about custody and our court case, the children will be pulled into this litigation and preoccupied with worries and doubts about their future and our love for them. That's not in their best interests."

It is also important that criticism of the other parent be balanced. If the other parent dearly loves the children but is inexperienced in relating to them, give the other parent credit for that love. For example, you can say, "I know that John dearly loves the children, but I'm not sure he knows how to properly relate to them as a parent." Or, you might say, "John has been a hard worker and a good provider, but I am concerned that his work hasn't left him much time to learn how to deal with children and meet their needs."

This is so much more effective than, "John loves his job more than he does me or the children."

Most important, if the children are young or even preteen, don't insist that the evaluator ask the children with whom they want to live. At best it gives the impression that you have been discussing custody with the child, and, at worst, it gives the impression that you may be trying to program a child to parrot your views to the evaluator. If the children are teenagers or mature preteens, you may safely say something like, "Perhaps the children can tell you more about that," and then drop the subject. The evaluator knows, without being reminded, that an interview with an older child is probably necessary.

You and Your Child Meet Together With the Evaluator

Meeting with you and your child together, without the other parent, will allow the evaluator to assess your relationship with the child and to compare that direct observation with your description of the relationship. It is an opportunity to assess your strengths and weaknesses as a parent. The evaluator may remain in the same room with you or watch from another room through a one-way mirror. If you do not have custody of the child, it may be helpful if you can arrange to bring the child to the meeting so that by the time that you arrive at the evaluator's office the child has an opportunity to adjust to being with you.

On the other hand, if you are unable to spend time with the child before the meeting, do not be overly concerned about an attempt by the other parent to program the child to be fearful of you at the meeting. If you have a close and loving relationship with your child, nothing the other parent can say or do will affect a young child beyond the first few minutes of the interview. An effort by one parent to make a child fearful of the other parent in order to cause a meeting with the evaluator to go poorly will not only fail, but it will backfire, bringing suspicion on the parent who sought to alienate the child from you. For example, the child may be very tentative toward you, or even appear to be frightened of you at first, but after a few minutes become loving, warm, and joyful toward you. The evaluator will likely conclude that this latter stage represents your true relationship with the child, and that the other parent did something to make the child initially insecure with you.

If the other parent is fearful and insecure about your relationship with the child, the child may mirror those fears for a short time into the meeting. However, whether the child's initial insecurity was from deliberate alienation or merely the insecurity of the custodial parent, a question has been raised about that parent's ability to support a relationship with you in an appropriate way. And that raises questions about that parent's general parenting ability.

Moreover, if the evaluator sees the child delivered to you by the custodial parent, and the child is tentative or standoffish at first, but runs joyfully to you when the custodial parent has left, the evaluator may conclude that the custodial parent has led the child to believe that the child is not free to have a close relationship with you. It will be evident that the child acted in a way to please the custodial parent until that parent could no longer see the child's real feelings for you. A scenario like this may cause the evaluator to suspect that the custodial parent is, consciously or unconsciously, unable or unwilling to support the child's relationship with you.

Before the time of the meeting, you will want to give some thought to how you can best interact with the child during the meeting. You may want to play a game that the child has enjoyed in the past, share a short story with the child, or bring paper and crayons so that you can draw together. You should know what the child will be comfortable doing. If you decide to use this opportunity to spend some conversation time getting caught up on events in the child's life since you were last together, keep in mind that you'll get more information from the child with open-ended questions (those that can't be answered "yes" or "no"). Remember that the evaluator wants to see you set limits if necessary. If the child is demanding or bossy or disobedient toward you, the evaluator may conclude that the child is acting in that way because you have allowed such conduct in the past. Thus, you must set limits during the meeting if necessary. You should be able to do so in a calm, firm, but loving way. If your child is running about the office making noise or being destructive as you and the evaluator seek to have a brief conversation, if you do not put an end to the conduct by bringing the child up on your lap or putting the child in a chair, or focusing the child's attention on something less annoying, the evaluator will justifiably question your ability and willingness to set reasonable limits.

Tell the Truth; Don't Exaggerate

Any time the evaluator comes to believe that you have been untruthful, your case is significantly damaged. The inability to be truthful may cause the evaluator to believe that you are over-invested in the outcome of the litigation and focused on its effect on you rather than on your children's best interests. The evaluator may wonder whether you will be unreliable or untrustworthy in your care of your children. Indeed, lying can suggest personality traits or disorders that limit your ability to care for a child properly. But the most damaging aspect of being caught in a lie is that from that point forward the evaluator will no longer presume that what you say is accurate. If, for example, you deny that you have a problem with alcohol and the evaluator finds two recent convictions for driving under the influence (in a printout of your criminal history obtained from law enforcement), the evaluator will thereafter doubt the validity of everything you say. If you allege that the children are fearful of the other parent, but the children exhibit no fear whatever in a meeting with the other parent in the evaluator's office, your judgment or veracity will be placed in doubt. Such contradictions will lead the evaluator to doubt whatever you may say thereafter in describing your parenting abilities or those of the other parent.

You also should not exaggerate by drawing improbable inferences from facts that may be correct. It casts doubt not so much on your veracity but on your judgment and the extent to which you may be overinvested in the outcome of the case. For example, if an active child returns from visitation with a cut or a scratch or bruise on an arm or leg, and the custodial parent immediately concludes that the child has been neglected or abused, that parent's case has been hurt. The parent who makes an allegation of sexual abuse of a child based upon what every good parent should know is diaper rash will be mistrusted in other conclusions. Whenever you have any question about whether an injury was caused by more than an unavoidable accident, talk to your pediatrician for an opinion.

It is also damaging to your case to deny the obvious. Even if a parent forthrightly admits to two recent convictions for driving under the influence, that person will hurt his case if he then tries to convince the evaluator that he doesn't have a problem with alcohol.

He does, and what is more important, he likely always will. The evaluator and the judge both have training in the signs and treatment of alcoholism. You are much better off admitting you have a problem and indicating that you are, or will be in a day or so, enrolled in a treatment program. Such a response, if carried out, shows a strength of character that will be admired by both the evaluator and the judge.

Whose Child Is It?

A word about how you refer to your child when talking with the evaluator or testifying in court. You should always refer to the child as "our" child rather than "my" child. It may seem a small thing, but "my child" not only has almost a proprietary ring to it, it does not recognize the rights and role of the other parent. Not all evaluators and judges may be bothered or offended by continued references to "my child," but you don't know the feelings or sensitivities of either your evaluator or judge, so it makes no sense to risk appearing to exclude the other parent from your thoughts about the child.

Private Versus Public Evaluation

In many states the court's custody evaluator is a mental health professional working as an employee of the court or the county, or may have a private practice under contract with the county to do custody evaluations. These evaluations are funded largely at taxpayer expense. Depending on the size of the county, the list of contractors to whom custody matters are assigned may be quite long or may consist of only one or two professionals. While those parents who can pay will normally be charged a fee for work by these publicly-funded professionals, it is usually only a fraction of what a mental health professional in private practice will charge for a custody evaluation.

When Is a Private Evaluator to Be Preferred?

Thus the question arises, when should one parent, through his or her attorney, seek the agreement of the other parent to take the custody issue to a "private" rather than a "public" sector evaluator?

It is unlikely that the judge will have the authority or inclination to refer a custody dispute to a private evaluator unless the parties agree to such a referral and agree to pay the charges involved, or unless the party seeking the referral offers to pay all of the evaluator's fee.

There are at least three advantages to private evaluation. First, the parents are permitted —if they can agree — to choose the person who will do the evaluation. If you are referred to a pool of court or county employees or contractors, it is unlikely that you will have any say in which person does your evaluation. If you are in one of the very few jurisdictions that permits you to challenge one evaluator before the evaluation process begins, you still cannot choose your evaluator. You will be given the next evaluator in the rotation or one who is appointed by the judge to replace the challenged evaluator. The internal procedures of the pool will determine the choice of evaluator for your custody case. With a private evaluator, you and the other parent can review the qualifications of a number of private evaluators before making the choice. When you are able to make such a selection, your choice of the attorney who represents you looms very important indeed. You need an attorney familiar with the quality of work, as well as the tendencies, preferences, and biases of almost any local evaluator who might be considered for your case. Such an attorney can give you sound advice on which evaluators do quality work with a high degree of fairness and objectivity. Your attorney should also know generally how the evaluators stand in relation to one another in terms of their charges. Fees for this work can range from $95 per hour to $350 per hour, and a higher fee does not necessarily indicate better quality work. Higher fees do normally indicate the amount of professional education and training an evaluator has, with child psychiatrists (medical doctors) and psychologists (Ph.D.'s) charging more than licensed social workers and marriage, family and child counselors (M.A. or equivalent). A higher degree from a recognized institution assures you of an amount and level of clinical training that is not available to those holding only a master's degree, but it is not a guarantee of better judgment or greater objectivity.

A second reason to prefer a private evaluator is that the private evaluator normally has more time to devote to a difficult or complicated case. It is not my intention to discount in any way the very excellent work done by public sector employees and contractors. However, they are overburdened by very large caseloads in most jurisdictions, and many cases have deadlines to be met. They often cannot be as thorough in their work as a private evaluator. Certain cases and issues should go to a private evaluator if the parties can possibly afford it. A relocation or "move-away" case, wherein a custodial parent wishes to move the children across the country or to another state or county, should go to private evaluation if feasible. Such a move has the potential to dramatically alter the nature of the relationship between the children and the parent who is left behind. It may be necessary to evaluate carefully the extent to which the children are bonded to the noncustodial parent, or to carefully assess the weight to be accorded to the preference of an older child not to move. It may be necessary to evaluate educational and extracurricular opportunities in the area to which the proposed move will be made. Conferences with local teachers and coaches may be appropriate. A relocation case takes far more time to investigate thoroughly than the average custody dispute.

Cases in which one parent has accused the other of sexually molesting a child, and the accused parent vehemently denies the charge, require a high level of clinical skill, experience, and the judgment to determine whether the allegation is probably true or false. The judge and evaluator cannot assume that such a charge made in the context of a divorce is probably true. Such an assumption is justified when children make charges against neighbors, relatives, or strangers. But in divorce cases where one parent charges the other parent or a relative or new mate of the other parent with molesting the child, it is your author's experience that the probability of the truth of the charge is established in less than 50 percent of the cases in which the charge is made. In such a case, a psychological evaluation which includes psychological testing is likely to be very helpful. That can be done only by a licensed psychologist. (Psychiatrists do not do, and are not trained to do, testing. They may on occasion farm the work out to a psychologist if they think that testing will be useful in getting at the truth.) A private evaluator may also have more time to seek the assistance of the judge or work with the child's attorney, if one has been appointed, to protect the child from numerous intrusive interviews by law enforcement, social workers, physicians, and child therapists hired by the parents.

Finally, cases of suspected parental alienation are best handled by a private evaluator. To determine whether a child is being subtly taught to disrespect or fear the other parent, or whether the fear arises from the inappropriate conduct of the other parent, takes many hours of interviews with both parents as well as the child. In addition, it requires an understanding of the symptoms and dynamics of alienation, and a careful psychological evaluation of the parent accused of alienation efforts to determine if the parent is unable to separate that parent's needs from those of the child. This normally takes clinical skills at the Ph.D. level.

That brings me to the third reason for preferring a private evaluation in certain cases. As a rule, psychologists or psychiatrists in private practice have far more clinical training than public sector employees. Mental health professionals in the public sector usually have only a master's degree and may or may not be licensed by the state. In some areas they are probation officers with an understanding of criminal and antisocial behavior, but little formal training in the emotional needs and behavior of children. Indeed, in some areas, public sector evaluators may hold no advanced degrees whatever.

A private evaluation could cost you between $2,000 and $10,000 depending upon the complexity of the case and the fee schedule of the evaluator. Even in the difficult cases described above, an evaluation in the public sector will *probably* produce the same result as that done by a highly qualified and objective private evaluator. *But not always.* And if the public evaluator reaches a conclusion that you and your attorney believe is flawed or unjustified, then you may be put to the expense of hiring a private therapist to review and render an opinion on the work of the public sector evaluator. The judge will not give you a second evaluation at public expense. Thus you may feel more secure starting out with a private evaluation. Unless you and your spouse choose someone whom the judge believes to be unreliable, the judge will make that person the court's own custody expert.

DO'S AND DON'TS

Do . . .

• Insist on knowing whether any mediation you attend is *real mediation* or whether the mediator is also an *evaluator* who will make a recommendation to the judge if you and the other parent fail to reach an agreement.

• Be prompt to your evaluation appointment and dress appropriately.

• Prior to the evaluation, think about your responses to questions you are likely to be asked and how you will describe your relationship with your child.

• Admit the parenting strengths of the other party.

• Frame your answers to questions in terms of the child's needs and best interests. Never talk about how much you enjoy or need the child.

• State criticisms of the other parent in terms of "concerns."

• If you and your child are meeting with the evaluator, and if you do not have custody at that time, try to bring the child to the meeting with you.

• Plan how you will interact with the child in the presence of the evaluator so as to best show your relationship with the child.

• Be sure your check in payment to the evaluator is good. A bounced check won't be in your favor when the report is prepared.

Don't . . .

• Try never to cancel an appointment with the evaluator, and absolutely never simply fail to show up.

• Don't ramble or go off on tangents; answer questions succinctly but completely, and answer only the question asked.

• Don't cry inappropriately during the evaluation.

• Don't ever conceal the fact that you have been a victim of physical abuse.

• Don't ever insist that the evaluator ask the children for a preference.

• If the other parent will not permit you to bring the child to a meeting with the evaluator, don't be concerned that the other parent will program the child against you so that the meeting will not go well. It can't be done. Such an attempt will backfire on the other parent.

• Don't draw unreasonable inferences from benign facts.

• Don't refer to the child as "my" child but as "our" child.

• Don't let your interview become a litany of your criticisms of the other parent to the exclusion of your strength as a caretaker.

3.

The Role of Attorneys in Custody Litigation

Many parents consider the possibility of handling custody proceedings without legal counsel, citing costs, escalation of hostilities, difficulty in finding an attorney, and a preference for self-reliance, among their reasons. Believe me, family court judges have heard all the arguments for such a decision. Before you decide, however, please read the discussion in this chapter. You may change your mind.

Do You Need an Attorney to Represent You?

Everyone involved in custody litigation is better off with a capable attorney than without one. Persons representing themselves are often called *"pro pers"* (my preference, and short for *in propria persona*), or *"in pro se"* in the legal community. Attorneys know the rules of procedure, both state and local. *Pro pers* do not know those rules, and often make costly procedural errors. An attorney is experienced in focusing the evidence on subjects the judge is interested in because they are relevant to the issue before the court. *Pro pers* often waste much of their time on matters that are irrelevant to the decision the judge must make. Moreover, an attorney is normally better organized and a more articulate speaker than the untrained litigant. An experienced attorney has a courtroom manner developed over the years that presumably has served the attorney well in a courtroom setting.

One of the most important and yet overlooked benefits of having an attorney is that the attorney "hides the parent's warts" from the judge. A mother may be absolutely consumed with inappropriate anger, but so long as the attorney is presenting the case and the client is sitting quietly, the judge doesn't see the anger. The father may have inappropriate feelings of emotion or victimization that the judge will not see. The judge will not see a client's inability to stay on the subject or to state logical and coherent thoughts. Moreover, many family law motions are done by what are called "offers of proof." That is, the client is sworn and then the attorney states in narrative form what the client's testimony would be were the client called to the witness stand and interrogated in the traditional question-and-answer form. After the offer of proof is completed, the client states that such would be her testimony and that it is true. This saves much time on a crowded court calendar. Only during what is usually brief cross-examination by the other attorney is there a chance for the client's inappropriate emotions to show through. Even clients who testify in the traditional manner find it far easier to keep in mind the attorney's admonishment against a display of anger or hostility during a given period of testimony than to appear emotionally proper through the many frustrations that arise when you try to present your case without counsel. In many cases I have seen *pro pers* show the worst possible attitudes about the other parent and reveal characteristics that diminish the *pro per*'s ability to be a good parent. I then look over at the other parent, sitting quietly at counsel table while the attorney calmly presents the case and I wonder, "How would that other parent come across if there were not an attorney here to present the case?"

But, if the attorney is to assist the client in that way, the client must sit calmly at counsel table and let the attorney present the case. Some clients insist on raising their hands and asking "May I say something?," as if the attorney is not as convincing as they will be or is not presenting the case properly. They normally do not help their case at all and often do great damage by the attitude they reveal in saying their "something." Clients who are continually clawing at the attorney's shoulder giving advice or commenting on someone's testimony often come across as having poor judgment, as defensive, as overly emotionally invested in the case, or as absolutely frantic. It is my view that the attorneys who do the best work in court are those who have very busy practices, who don't need any particular case, and who make it very clear to the client early on that if the client can't sit calmly at counsel table with hands folded while the case is being presented, the client should find another lawyer. This is a sound practice, although the client should feel free to write a note once in a while that the attorney will turn to when the attorney believes it appropriate.

Finally, the attorney knows the law, both the law that applies to the case as well as the rules of evidence. When an attorney objects to the question of a *pro per* by saying, "objection, no foundation laid," the *pro per* has no idea what the attorney means or what must be done to get around the objection. Moreover, many judges do not believe that it is proper to help the *pro per* by explaining the objection.

Whatever you do, don't hire an attorney to come to court with you only as a legal advisor who sits there while you present the case. The experience of judges with such litigants is that they are very self-centered and lack almost any ability to trust. Neither characteristic is very helpful to a parent in raising children. If you cannot afford to have an attorney come to court with you, but you can afford to have an attorney help you with the paperwork and explain what will be expected of you in court, then by all means retain such an attorney.

A capable attorney will also tell you when not to respond to a provocation that might touch an emotional chord in you. The attorney can also tell you when some conduct you plan to engage in will be seen as provocative by the judge. For example, assume in a high-conflict case that the father moves out of the family home into a place of his own in order to reduce emotional stress on the parents and the children. A divorce action is filed but the mother does not seek restraining orders to prevent his return because he has no plans to return and she wants to save money and not be provocative. About nine months later, funds are short, and it is difficult for the husband to continue to pay rent on a separate dwelling, so he decides to move back in without court permission. The wife's capable attorney will tell him that such an action will bring a motion for a restraining order that will increase legal fees, that the motion will probably be granted, and the judge will look upon the father's return as provocative.

In a close case, the attorney's capability can affect the result. Even if you do not obtain primary custody of the children, the capable attorney may well obtain greater access to the children than you might otherwise have received. On the other hand, there are some attorneys whose skills are so poor that they will actually diminish your chances of obtaining what you believe is a favorable result.

As emphasized in the introduction of this book, no attorney can bring a favorable result if the facts do not support that result. If you retain an attorney with the idea that, regardless of the facts, he or she will bring you a favorable result by extraordinary courtroom technique (e.g., brilliant cross-examination and sheer force of personality), you will be disappointed and will be changing attorneys early on. This makes good television drama but seldom happens in real trials before judges. Indeed, even if you can find and afford one of the very best divorce lawyers in the county, your spouse will be able to hire someone just as capable. If you are the high earner of the two parents, in all states you will likely be ordered to contribute to the other parent's attorney fees so that the other parent can have counsel with skill comparable to your lawyer's. Judges by-and-large believe in a level playing field in divorce cases.

How to Choose an Attorney

What are the characteristics that you want in an attorney? Here are ten suggestions for your consideration:

1. Obviously you want someone whose hourly rate is within reason for a person with your income and your size of estate. If you ask the attorney for an estimate of the total cost of the case based on your description of the disputes, double or triple the answer and ask yourself if you can afford that sum alone, or with some assistance from the other parent. The costs of divorce cases always exceed the early estimates of the attorney. You should also avoid an attorney who wants an unreasonable retainer fee to be paid in advance of any work commencing on the case. For example, some attorneys demand retainer fees in the neighborhood of $10,000, and require that you agree that the retainer fee is non-refundable under any circumstances. The attorney keeps the retainer even if you reconcile before a single paper is filed with the court or if you discharge the attorney for good cause. A non-refundable portion of the retainer of $1,500 to $2,000 in order to

show your good faith and to cover the costs of setting up a file is reasonable. Some litigants retain an attorney just to intimidate their spouse but have no intention of carrying through with the divorce. However, an attorney who insists that the entire $10,000 retainer be nonrefundable under any circumstances does not have your best interests at heart.

2. As will be reiterated throughout this book, you need representation by a local attorney with substantial custody case experience with local judges and custody evaluators. You should not assume that because an attorney has a thriving practice in divorce litigation, the attorney has substantial experience in custody cases. A significant number of attorneys do not like custody litigation and only occasionally take on a custody case.

3. You would be wise to retain a certified family law specialist if one is available, unless you are absolutely confident that the uncertified attorney you choose has the requisite experience needed to represent you well. Unfortunately, only nine states have laws that specifically provide for the certification of attorneys as specialist and require that the attorneys pass an examination in order to obtain and advertise the status of certified specialist in a given area of law. However, a number of states allow an attorney to advertise as a specialist in family law if that is indeed the truth — but in those states there is no examination to insure a minimum level of competency in the field. A minority of states prohibit the advertising of a specialty. Family law is now considered by some to be the most complex of all areas of law. One needs a substantial knowledge of tax law, of the rules of small business evaluation, pension evaluation, stock option evaluation, and real property evaluation. It may be that custody law is less complex than the law related to property and financial issues, but litigants seldom have only a custody issue to resolve.

4. Probably the most important characteristic of a skillful and capable family lawyer is that he or she has established a reputation for integrity and judgment with the judge. While a reputation for integrity is helpful to an attorney in all aspects of a case, nowhere is it more important than when you seek an emergency order without a hearing, based solely upon affidavits or declarations. If, in past cases with the judge, the allegations in the declarations of your attorney's clients have turned out to be accurate when a hearing is later held, the chance of the judge signing your proposed order

is increased fivefold. If the judge believes that your attorney is one of those who serves up to the judge whatever the client is willing to swear to and does not carefully question the client concerning veracity of the allegations made and how they can be proven, then you are not apt to obtain an *ex parte* order without a hearing.

5. Your attorney should be willing to prepare the case herself rather than having preparation done by paralegals or junior attorneys. In a word, you want to avoid a "divorce mill." I use that term to describe a practice in which an attorney interviews the client initially, but the case is then prepared for trial by underlings in the office who do all of the discovery (by way of subpoenas, depositions, or requests to produce documents) and all of the legal research and writing necessary for motions and trials. The attorney only sees the file the day before a court hearing at best, and only after arriving in court at worst. I have seen instances of cases that have been very competently prepared for trial by staff persons in the office, but the attorney presenting the case in court did not know the contents of the file. This is especially damaging if the attorney is in a settlement conference. Unless the attorney is conversant with the strengths and weaknesses of the evidence and the witnesses for each side, she cannot properly evaluate an offer to settle the case that would end the expenditure of attorney fees and bring the case to a conclusion.

6. You want an attorney who will return your phone calls within a reasonable period of time. Failure to return phone calls is probably the most frequent complaint made by clients of attorneys. If you do not abuse the right to call the attorney, your occasional calls should be returned within 24 hours. If your attorney is in trial or otherwise unable to return your call, the call should be returned by someone sufficiently knowledgeable with the file to be able to answer your questions. On the other hand, the attorney has a right to be assured that you will not make incessant and unnecessary telephone calls. In family law cases, some clients try to use the attorney as a therapist to give them emotional support. That is improper and is not fair to the attorney.

7. You may want an attorney to keep you involved in the progress of your case by sending you copies of all pleadings and correspondence in the case. Some attorneys do this as a matter of routine unless the client requests otherwise. Generally, the more a client is involved in the case, the better the communication will be with the attorney.

8. Every client is in need of an attorney who can answer the client's questions in a way the client can understand. It is not your job to educate yourself so that you will better understand the attorney, or to accept an answer you do not understand. It is the attorney's job to make the answer both accurate and understandable to you. If at the initial interview you do not understand something the attorney has said, you should say that you do not understand and ask for clarification. The attorney is entitled to have an opportunity to clarify and you are entitled to an answer that is clear to you. If you cannot seem to get one, you should consider retaining another attorney. Without clear communication, the attorney-client relationship is likely to break down.

9. It would also be helpful if your attorney had a cordial and working relationship with the other parent's attorney. Nothing can waste money faster than two feuding attorneys who are more focused on their own hostilities than on the case. Of course, some attorneys get along with no one, and the other parent may have had the bad judgment to hire such a person. However, if only one attorney you interview has a problem with the other parent's attorney and everyone else finds the choice quite acceptable, maybe that attorney you interviewed is the one who can't get along with anyone. Moreover, you want the other parent to be well represented. A *pro per* with no concept of what is a reasonable offer of settlement, or who fails to produce documents when requested, will drive up your legal fees.

10. It is also helpful if you find an attorney who has respect for the local system. An attorney who has nothing but complaints about the local judges and the custody evaluators may well be an attorney who has been notably unsuccessful in the system or even one who is considered by judges and evaluators to create more problems than he solves.

How Will You Know If an Attorney Has Sufficient Experience to Handle Your Custody Case?

A local attorney experienced in custody matters will know the answers to certain questions about practice in the local courts. For example, is mediation required as part of the court process? Is the mediation confidential or will the mediator make a recommendation to the judge if the parties do not reach an agreement? If mediation is confidential, who acts as the evaluator when mediation fails?

The attorney should also be able to give you a thumbnail sketch of the various stages of custody litigation, by explaining when mediation takes place, when settlement conferences will be set, how long it will take to get to a hearing on temporary custody and then to get to a trial on the issue of permanent custody. The attorney would know how often local judges appoint attorneys or guardians *ad litem* for children, if at all, and whether psychological evaluations and testing are occasionally ordered by the local judges and in what types of cases. Finally, the attorney should know some of the names of the persons to whom the judge might refer the case for a custody evaluation, both in the public and private sector.

Whom Should You Not Hire?

From the discussion thus far, readers will surely conclude that they should not hire out-of-county attorneys who do not practice regularly in the local court, attorneys who overreach on their retainer fee agreement, who turn the entire preparation of the case over to paralegals or others, or who will not even guarantee you that he or she will be the person who accompanies you to court. There are other characteristics that would not be disqualifying in themselves, but, like uncorroborated criticism of the other parent's attorney, should be at least a small red flag. Beware the attorney who guarantees you a certain result in any portion of your case. The system is just too fraught with unknowns to make such promises. If an attorney never disagrees with anything you say about your case and the way in which you wish to proceed and the goals you wish to achieve, you may want to ponder how likely it is that you are correct in everything you say and whether this attorney is willing to be candid with you. Finally, you may want to be skeptical of an attorney who does not give you any indication of what the attorney expects from a client. The attorney is bound to have some expectations that the client is expected to meet, and you have a right to know these in advance of making the selection of an attorney.

How Do You Choose an Attorney to Represent You?

Many people seeking an attorney to represent them in litigation simply get the name of someone from a friend, their barber or hairdresser, a banker, or some other social or business acquaintance.

These are not good referral sources. It's likely that they (or someone they know) has been a client of the attorney they recommend and their evaluation of the attorney's ability is based upon that relationship. Unfortunately, however, clients tend not to be good judges of their attorneys' ability. They are notoriously result-oriented. If the result of the litigation was what they wanted, they see their attorney as almost infallible. If they believe that they lost the case, they do not see the attorney as having done good work. Yet judges and court staff see instances all of the time where the case of the prevailing side was very poorly presented and the attorney for the losing side took an almost impossible factual situation and very nearly turned it into a victory. The fact that one side prevailed does not necessarily mean that the attorney for that side was fully prepared, had done the necessary research to have a thorough grasp of the legal issues in the case, or made a good choice of who to call as witnesses.

The persons who know which attorneys are respected by the judges for their integrity and skill are people that work in courtrooms: *clerks, bailiffs,* and *court reporters.* If you have a friend who is acquainted with anyone who works in the court system, that person can either give your friend the names of three or four highly qualified attorneys or will know someone else in the court system who can. *Mental health professionals* who do evaluations in custody cases, whether they are in the public or private sector, are another excellent source of information about attorneys. They have watched many attorneys in court and been called as a witness by or cross-examined by a number of them. They have a general knowledge of the fee schedule of various attorneys. Moreover, almost any mental health professional in a county will either be acquainted with someone who does forensic custody work, or will know someone who is so acquainted. *Attorneys who do not do family law* may also be a source of referrals although they do not have the knowledge of court staff or mental health professionals, and there is always the danger of getting caught up in a "good old boy" network or being referred to someone else in the office who does practice family law. And of course you never want an attorney friend who does not do significant family law to represent you "as a favor." Both you and that attorney are asking for trouble. The offer should be declined even if the services are to be rendered without charge. (Remember the ten characteristics you *do* want!)

If the avenues for obtaining referrals suggested above are not productive, *family lawyers* themselves are very knowledgeable about the quality of work of their colleagues. You might consider obtaining the name of a certified specialist from a friend or finding a specialist in the telephone book and in the course of the interview you can ask for the names of three or four attorneys to whom that attorney refers cases when a conflict of interest develops. Most attorneys will give you an honest answer to that question and will not be offended that you appear to be shopping around. If you ask that question of two or three attorneys and one person seems to be on everyone's referral list, you might want to interview that attorney.

Finally, you can always pick out the names of three or four certified family law specialists from the *Yellow Pages*, interview them, and see what other names may come up along the way. I do not think you should interview any fewer than three attorneys, no matter how impressed you are at the first interview. In addition, it is not a good idea to make your choice while you are in the attorney's office for the initial interview. You will need time to go over the fee agreement carefully. What is the nature of the retainer you are being asked to pay? Will it be applied against future work? When it is exhausted, will you be billed monthly or are you expected to pay another sum equal to the first? What funds or property that you may be awarded in the dissolution will the attorney have a lien on, if any, for fees then owing? Will you be charged for telephone calls? Is there a minimum charge per call? At what rate does the attorney bill for the time of paralegals? For other attorneys in the office? For secretarial time? If your attorney is discussing your case with another attorney in the office, are you billed for the time of both? It is not at all improper to seek the advice of independent counsel if you are uncertain about the legal implications of some of the wording in the fee agreement. It may cost you between $500 and $1,000 to interview four attorneys if they all charge for initial interviews, but if a custody dispute is involved, it will be a small percentage of your total fees.

Changing Attorneys — Beware of the Stigma Involved

If you discharge your attorney because you don't agree with the result of the first hearing or so, you may be making a serious mistake. Your attorney did not create the facts. You may have been very competently represented despite the adverse ruling. Rather than discharging the attorney, you might sit down with him and see if he can give you some insight into the reasons for the judge's ruling and what you might do to be more successful in the future.

There is one circumstance in which you might reasonably discharge the attorney. If the attorney told you or led you to believe that you were going to get everything you wanted at a given hearing, then you have a right to question the attorney's judgment. As you know from earlier in this chapter, you should never have retained an attorney who guaranteed or promised anything, and so it may well be wise to find other counsel as soon as possible. Even if no overt promise is made, the attorney who allows the client to get pumped up with a feeling that any litigation, or even a single motion, is a slam dunk is guilty of the worst kind of lawyering. In a custody matter, it is outrageous. Judges and mediators hold many settlement conferences every week, and they are justifiably annoyed when they see a client come to a settlement conference with no concept or thought that the judge may not see things the client's way on every single issue. These clients go through enormous psychic pain when reality is unexpectedly thrust upon them and they are asked to make major concessions in a matter of minutes. The judge cannot help but suspect that the attorney painted an unrealistically rosy picture in order to obtain a retainer fee, and then has left it up to the judge to bring the client back to reality. On the other hand, result-oriented clients who retain the attorney who paints the rosiest scenario of the outcome are certainly not free from blame for their predicament when things go poorly.

If the judge's file reflects that you changed attorneys after an early adverse ruling, the judge will suspect that you may be the type of litigant with sufficiently poor judgment to believe that the right attorney will make all of the problems with the case go away. This is especially likely if you have discharged someone whom the judge considers to be an excellent family lawyer.

The litigant who changes attorneys two or three times almost invariably becomes stigmatized as a difficult and obstreperous person who will not take the advice of others. If you doubt that judges hold that view, you may be convinced at a hearing when the other parent's attorney points out in her first sentence to the judge that you are on your third or fourth attorney. That opposing attorney knows how judges view litigants who change attorneys several times. Indeed many of these people wind up *in pro per* because they cannot find another attorney willing to take their case at any price. These attorneys who refuse to take a case with three or four prior attorneys hold the belief that the litigant who changes attorneys several times probably cannot get along with anyone.

Suppose Your Attorney Wants to Withdraw from the Case?

Let the attorney withdraw! If you have been unable to keep your bill current and you have not given the attorney a lien on property to secure payment, the attorney is legally and morally entitled to withdraw. Your attorney should not be required to finance your case. An attorney who does not require a client to keep the bill current has a client without the motivation to settle that most clients have. As a result, the unpaid bill just gets bigger.

If the attorney wants to withdraw because you will not take her advice, or you and the attorney have a different concept of how the case should be conducted, or you sense that the attorney feels that you are a difficult client, you should let the attorney withdraw, rather than forcing the attorney to bring a motion in court and ask to judge for permission to withdraw. Some attorneys — and perhaps in violation of their duty under the rules of professional conduct — spell out in detail in their declaration the conduct of the client that has led to the motion: failure to return telephone calls, to respond to letters, to notify the attorney of a change of address, or to produce relevant documents requested by the other side. When this happens, the file has been irrevocably tainted against you. Indeed, in a motion for attorney fees, the opposing attorney may quote from your former attorney's declaration. Even if your attorney says no more than something as benign as that you have been "uncooperative," that is going to raise questions about your conduct with any judge or custody evaluator who reviews the file.

You allow your attorney to withdraw by signing a substitution of attorneys. That document reveals nothing other than that the two of you came to an agreed-upon parting of the ways. If your attorney mails the document to you, sign it and return it. However, before you sign the document you are entitled to know whether any hearings are pending of which you are unaware, to know the status of your bill — whether you owe funds or are entitled to a partial refund of a retainer — and to know when you can pick up your file so that you can take it to another attorney if you wish. The rules of professional conduct require your attorney to turn over your file to you or an attorney of your choosing within a reasonable period of time. It cannot be withheld until your bill is paid.

DO'S AND DON'TS

Do . . .

• Hire an attorney to represent you in court if you can afford it.

• Hire a local attorney with extensive custody experience.

• Ask a few questions, at your initial interview, that a local attorney experienced in custody cases should know the answers to.

• Conduct three or four interviews with certified family law specialists, if possible.

• Seek the names of respected local custody attorneys from court staff, forensic mental health professionals, and other family lawyers.

• Ask your attorney to send you copies of all correspondence and pleadings.

• Make sure you understand all aspects of the retainer agreement before you sign it.

• Try to choose an attorney who has a cordial relationship with the other parent's attorney.

• Prior to signing a substitution of attorneys, (1) clarify the status of your bill, (2) determine when you or another attorney you have chosen can pick up your file, and (3) learn whether any court appearances are pending of which you are unaware.

Don't . . .

• Don't try to talk directly to the judge if you are represented in court by an attorney.

• Don't chatter at your attorney when he or she is presenting your case.

• Don't ever take an attorney to court only as a "legal advisor."

• Don't choose an attorney who charges a large nonrefundable retainer fee.

• Don't get all your names of attorneys to interview from friends or business acquaintances.

• Don't go to an attorney who runs a divorce mill.

• Don't sign a retainer agreement at the time of your first interview with an attorney.

• Don't discharge your attorney solely because you don't like an early ruling by the judge.

• Don't change attorneys more than once.

• Don't outright refuse to sign a substitution of attorneys.

4.

Protecting Your Child

All children are adversely affected to some extent by the separation of their parents. They have a deep sense of loss for even the most inadequate parent, and they long to have their parents back together again. Moreover, many children blame themselves for the divorce. The loss of a parent affects a child's ability to trust. Children of divorce often harbor fears that will affect their ability to trust if the fears are realized: loss of their home; loss of friends; loss of their standard of living. And they are very vulnerable to suggestion by either parent.

All parents worthy of the name want to protect their children as much as possible from these affects of a dissolution. How do you balance that goal with making your best case for custody? That's the issue we'll address in this chapter.

Protecting Your Child Will Not Hurt Your Custody Case

It will not adversely affect your custody case if you make an effort to protect your child from the possible long-term emotional damage many children experience during their parents' divorce. A sincere desire to protect your child may, however, reduce your ability to hurt the other parent. Vindictive parents — in their effort to inflict emotional pain on the other parent — often harm their children.

How best, then, to protect your child? The rules are quite simple.
• Do not disparage the other parent in any way in the presence of the child.
• Do not make any effort to thwart the other parent's time with the child.
• Do not communicate to the child overtly or simply by your anxiety or tone of voice that the child is not free to have a loving relationship with the other parent.
• Do not discuss any aspect of the court case with the child, or ask the child for a preference as to where the child wishes to live.
• Do not seek to alienate the child from the other parent by subtle ploys. For example, don't tell the child secrets that the child is not to disclose to the other parent. Don't schedule the child's favorite activity during the other parent's allotted time with the child and then tell the child that, but for the other parent, she would be able to engage in the favorite activity.
• Do not take the child to a therapist for the purpose of obtaining support for your case.
• Do not — and this is most important — try to deprive the other parent of your child, even if the other parent does so in an attempt to hurt you.

If you do anything that will harm your child, it may be uncovered by your evaluator and will hurt your chances of obtaining a favorable custody award. If the other parent criticizes you in the child's presence or seeks in other ways to alienate you from the child, simply continue to do what you know is right. The other's effort will fail.

Many mental health professionals believe — and your author shares this view — that if the parent under attack refuses to respond in kind, the effort to alienate a child from that parent will fail. Children are generally quite smart in these matters, and if your conduct does not justify the criticism, the child will not buy into it. (That is not to say it may not be emotionally harmful to the child.) It is only when you respond by joining the fray that your conduct, as seen by the child, gives support to the criticisms of the other parent. However, the alienation may succeed if you fail to give generously of your available time to the child. A child who believes he can depend on just one parent for care and protection may side with that parent because he fears losing his only source of care — even if that parent is attempting to alienate him from the other parent. Indeed, children will come to deny a parent's obvious faults if they believe that if the faults are discovered the child will lose the parent. A good example is the child who denies that the parent is drinking excessively each day when the child has both seen the drinking and complained about it.

If the child repeats to you things the other parent has said about you, a response such as "I'm sure your mom didn't mean that" is a response that your child instinctively knows is correct. If you have to give up a visitation so that the child can attend an activity that is important to the child, the child is certainly not hurt and you look very good in the eyes of the evaluator, who has seen and is quite sensitive to all of the alienation games. To protect your child from serious emotional damage you must assure the child, as many times and in as many ways as necessary, that both parents love the child, and that neither parent will abandon the child either emotionally or in terms of material needs.

How Do Most Parents Act?

Parents are not perfect, of course, and in a dissolution both are likely to engage in some amount of conduct that will harm the child emotionally to some degree. Most parents find it impossible to always be supportive of the other parent and to refrain from criticizing the other parent. Indeed, some parents find it difficult to control their expression of distrust for their former spouses. They may, for example, experience a great deal of anxiety near the time that the child is to be exchanged between the parents. (It is worth noting that recent studies indicate that parents who provoke conflict at the time of the exchanges of the child do serious and permanent emotional harm to the child.)

Nevertheless, while an occasional show of disdain for the other parent will be confusing for the child, it is a far cry from the unceasing campaign of spite and alienation that some parents wage. These are parents who take the child to multiple therapists, trying to find one who will be critical of the caregiving abilities of the other parent. Others will read the psychological evaluation of the other parent to the child. Some enmesh the child in the litigation, perhaps telling the child that the other parent does not care about the child because the support payments are frequently late or inadequate. And, of course, there are parents who conjure up false charges of molestation against the other parent as a way of limiting the accused's contact with the child. Such false accusers are seriously disordered individuals who cannot separate the child's needs from their own.

Extremes of misconduct such as these may leave a permanent emotional scar that will make it very difficult for that child to later establish a lasting relationship with another person, or to be an adequate parent or caretaker to a child. The offices of mental health professionals are filled with individuals working to heal the wounds of childhood.

The Symptoms of Emotional Damage

The short-term symptoms of emotional damage are usually obvious. The child, caught in a conflict between warring parents, and not wishing to offend either one, daily walks a tightrope between them. Over time, children of high-conflict divorce learn what pleases each of their parents and conduct themselves accordingly. They say what each parent wants to hear, and it is not unusual for the child to join in criticism of whichever parent is not present at the time. Indeed, it is common for such children to tell each parent that they want to live with *that* parent. All of the child's energy goes into surviving in the battle between the parents. Is it any wonder that teachers soon report an attention deficit and that school grades fall? Is it any surprise that the child shows great suppressed anger and starts to act aggressively toward playmates? Can you blame a child for being angry at being put in an impossible position by people over whom the child has no control?

The long-term emotional damage to children as a result of the improper conduct of their parents during a divorce inhibits their ability to lead happy and productive lives within the society. The alienated child will have a skewed view of adults and of the gender of the parent who is the victim of the alienation. The abandoned child will find it hard to fully trust as an adult, especially those who should be very close and deeply loved. Indeed some abandoned children may spend their early adult years in the unhealthy search for a mate who will serve in the role of the parent who has abandoned the child. The child who witnesses abuse, physical or verbal, is far more likely to so abuse family members later in life.

Children who walk a tightrope, telling each parent what that parent wants to hear, over time lose touch with their own true feelings and needs. They have lost part of their grasp on reality. Such a loss can produce serious emotional disorders that may — without serious therapeutic interventions — last a lifetime. At the least, it is likely that these children will find it difficult to establish a lifelong love relationship.

What Can Divorcing Parents Do to Protect Their Children?

In addition to refraining from the conduct described on page 54, there are a number of affirmative acts you and the other parent can do to reduce the emotional toll of your separation on the children. Once you have determined that a separation is certain and is imminent, you and the other parent should have a calm talk with all your children old enough to understand that their parents are separating. Explain to the children these key points:

• Despite the separation, you have respect for each other's parenting abilities.

• You simply feel that you will both be happier living apart.

• The separation is no one's fault, especially not the children's.

• You both love the children and will always love them.

• Both of you will continue to be close to them and to support them.

• They will spend lots of time with both parents, but for the time being the children will live primarily with (mom) (dad).

• You will work out a parenting plan or, if you disagree, a judge will order a parenting plan that is good for them.

• Neither parent will be able to afford what they could when they did not each have separate housing costs to pay, but hopefully this will only be temporary.

This first talk need not raise subjects like the possible need for the sale of the family home, or that the children will later be meeting one parent's new mate. Children better tolerate adverse news in measured doses.

Your children need someone to talk to, someone to whom they can reveal their true feelings even if they are not exhibiting symptoms of the stress of their parents' separation. Please understand that your children cannot and will not share these feelings with you or their other parent. They fear that there will be consequences if they say the wrong thing to a parent. Don't try to be their counselor (therapist) any more than you should try to be their swim or tennis coach. Such roles conflict with your role as a parent. A therapist will help the children keep their fears in perspective and prevent them from blaming themselves for the separation. The therapist can also help them not to hope unrealistically for a reconciliation of their parents (as most children do). The therapist will recommend to you whether or not your children are in need of therapy.

What Kind of Therapist Do Children of Separation Need?

Your children need a therapist who will serve each child individually and will accord them confidentiality. The therapist should not tell either parent what their child has said, but will give the parents an overview of how the child is doing and what the parents might do to better meet the child's needs. Your child needs a therapist who specializes in children, or for whom children compose at least 40 percent of the therapist's practice.

Under no circumstances should the therapist also be seeing either parent as a client. That would create a conflict of interest. The best interests of the children often diverge from the best interests of the parents. If the therapist has both a parent and the child as clients, whose interest shall the therapist favor? Indeed, competent therapists will not take on such a dual role.

The names of several competent child therapists can be obtained from custody evaluators who either work for the court or county or are under contract with the county to do custody evaluations.

The therapist should be chosen and approved by both parents since a therapist chosen unilaterally by one parent likely will be mistrusted by the other. The parents should agree, in a written statement approved by the court, that the therapist will not be called as a witness in the custody case. A child who suspects that the therapist will leak back to the parents what she has said, will most often tell the therapist what the parents want to hear rather than revealing her true feelings. Parents who know that the therapist may testify will seek to persuade the therapist of the merit of their own custody claims, rather than giving the therapist an honest appraisal of the children's emotional difficulties. Money spent on the therapist will be wasted in these circumstances.

If the parties can afford it, they should concentrate on finding a highly competent therapist with extensive experience with children, rather than concentrating on their insurance company's list of approved therapists. It is also a good idea to choose a fee-for-service therapist rather than one who works for an HMO or other managed care organization (MCO). First, the MCO has your premiums (the fee) in advance and is motivated to provide as little service as possible. My experience with Kaiser Permanente in Santa Clara County (California) is that there is a tendency to put a bandage on serious problems that need intensive treatment and to terminate treatment as soon as possible. Moreover, Kaiser and other HMOs put a limit —unrelated to the child's emotional needs — on the number of visits to which a child is entitled each year. The best child therapists find it intolerable to work under such limitations. While Kaiser maintains that the limit can be waived in an appropriate case, the policy itself reveals a non-supportive attitude toward psychotherapy.

Group therapy can be very helpful to children of divorce. There are programs in virtually every area of the country in which children meet with other children while the parents are meeting separately with experts in the needs of children of divorce. These group meetings can be very significant for the children who come to realize for the first time that they are not the only ones with the feelings of fear, guilt, and anger in relation to their parents' separation. Other children of divorce are going through the same experience of spending enormous amounts of energy in pleasing both parents and worrying about the future. They also realize that their peers are witnessing the same high level of conflict that they see almost daily.

The effect of this shared experience can be very therapeutic.

When Parents Are the Problem

Unfortunately, we judges are probably more pessimistic and cynical than others about the conduct of parents during divorce. Judges do not see the cases where the parents are working together to protect the children. Those cases never need a hearing. We are more likely to be called upon to bring a halt to conduct that is destructive to the emotional well-being of children. We see parent dispute over such things as who does the driving for visitation, at what location are the children to be exchanged, and whether the parent with whom the children reside is to be called the "primary custodial parent" or the "sole custodial parent." These are issues that are available for the parents' power struggle and have little or no effect on the children's best interests. We see moms who encourage the child to call their new mate "dad." We see parents who interrogate a child endlessly about events occurring in the other parent's home while the child was present. We see children witnessing physical violence, shouting, and name-calling between parents and between parents and their new mates. Or equally destructive, we see cases where a visitation schedule must be established in which the parents never come into contact with one another. Judges know that these children will find it a difficult struggle trying to grow up to be the loving, capable, caring, and independent adults that the parents hope they will be.

Among the most destructive of all conduct in which a parent can engage is the abduction of a child. It is an act based on vindictiveness and a warped view of the child's best interests. The goal of denying the other parent access to the child by removing the child is normally not successful. Local authorities usually locate and return children to the other parent within few weeks or months.

A rare exception to this which may obstruct recovery of the child is abduction to a foreign country that is not a signator to the Hague Conventions on international child custody (e.g., Iran, Israel, Libya, Pakistan). If the abduction is successful the child will be raised with false beliefs concerning the other parent and often the other parent's country and values.

The abduction of girls to certain Middle Eastern countries is especially tragic. They will be raised to believe that their role is to be subservient to men, and that it is improper to seek to achieve in their own right apart from their male companion. They will be denied a Western education if they are educated at all. It is unlikely that they will have certain basic comforts and securities that we in the West take for granted and for which so many Middle Easterners migrate to the West.

Protecting Your Child
From the Other Parent

None of us should be so naive as to believe that a parent need only encourage a relationship with the other parent in order to protect a child from serious psychological damage. At times a child needs protection from a parent who is damaging the child's emotional health. The problem is that it is often difficult to prove that a parent's conduct is detrimental to the child. Moreover, of course, the process of obtaining help from the court can be very expensive.

If you can establish that the conduct of the other parent is putting the child at risk for emotional harm, the judge can make orders that will protect a child. For example, the parent found to be harming the child can be limited to supervised visitation only. In many counties and states there are persons and companies in the private sector who offer, for a fee, to supervise visitation ordered by a court. Such supervisors range from those who will only supervise a visit of one hour at a single location to those who will accompany a parent and child to the beach, to a theme park, or on a full day's excursion that includes an airplane flight. Fee-based supervision, of course, is largely the prerogative of the well-to-do. The cost can range from $20 per hour up to $125 per hour (for a mental health professional). Depending on the financial circumstances of the parties and the reason that supervision is necessary, the court may order the supervised parent to pay the entire fee or may order the fee to be shared. Even in a county or state where supervision is provided by a public agency, there is likely to be a fee. However, public agencies seldom require the fee to be paid in advance as do almost all private supervisors, and thus parents of modest means can avail themselves of professional supervision.

If the parties cannot afford a professional supervisor, it is sometimes possible for the judge to find a relative of one of the parents willing to do the supervision. However, in many instances a relative of one parent is not acceptable to the other parent. This is often a justified position; the relative may have become firmly aligned with the related parent and would not do the supervision in an objective and fair manner.

If there is no relative willing and qualified to do the work for parties who cannot afford a professional supervisor, the judge is faced with choosing between unsupervised visitation and a de facto termination of all but telephone access. Judges are understandably reluctant to completely terminate a child's access to one parent for fear that the child will feel abandoned by that parent and suffer emotional harm as a result.

Of course, the major problem in obtaining an order for supervised visitation is the difficulty in proving that the other parent is damaging your child emotionally. In some cases, it is relatively easy to obtain a supervision order from the judge. In the case of alleged physical or sexual abuse, the judge will almost always terminate the accused parent's unsupervised access pending a hearing and investigation of the charges. If the charges are found to be substantiated, the termination will be extended for a much longer period. Likewise, it is not difficult to establish that an alcoholic or drug-addicted parent who has access to a vehicle puts a child at risk both emotionally and physically.

In cases of subtle forms of alienation and disparagement, the need for supervision is more difficult to prove. Some parents are either so selfish or emotionally disordered themselves that they simply will not (cannot?) stop an unceasing campaign of alienation or disparagement of the other parent. This situation is terribly emotionally damaging to a child. I have presided over cases in which children have commenced to have hallucinations or delusions as a result of this type of psychological manipulation by a parent.

Certain Persons Can Assist You in Proving Parental Alienation

There are certain steps that an innocent parent can take which may make the proof of the need for supervision easier in cases of alienation and disparagement. The child should be placed in therapy with a mental health professional approved by the court and/or the other parent. Over a series of sessions the child is almost certain to reveal to the therapist if a parent's conduct is harming or will harm the child if not stopped. While you don't want to embroil the therapist in the custody litigation for reasons discussed elsewhere, the therapist can communicate his or her concern to the custody evaluator who can then recommend to the judge supervised or suspended visitation.

It may also be helpful for an attorney to be appointed to represent a child you believe is being harmed by the verbal abuse of the other parent. Custody evaluators, especially those in the public sector, seldom have time the act as a caseworker and to see a child at regular intervals. On the other hand, the child's attorney may do just that and obtain a better picture of the pressures being brought to bear on your child. The most important work of a child's attorney is to immediately inform the judge or evaluator of any dangers to the well-being of the child-client.

Finally, you may find it helpful if a *special master* is appointed in the case. In this context, a special master is a mental health professional appointed and given the authority to resolve disputes between the parents over child-related issues. The special master allows the parties to resolve their disputes over vacations, health care, education, transportation, and other aspects of a parenting plan without the need to spend the money to return to court each time a dispute arises. An experienced special master who sees the parties several times may get a better handle on the dynamics of the relationship between the parents and the child than the judge or the custody evaluator, who have hundreds of cases a year to resolve. The use of mental health professionals as special masters (called *referees* in some jurisdictions) has become very popular in some parts of California and is beginning to slowly penetrate other jurisdictions as well. The judge may not have the authority to appoint a special master without the consent of both parents, but don't be certain that you can't get the consent of the offending parent. Parents who seek to alienate children from the other parent are often acting as they do as a result of long-standing personality disorders that do not allow them to see what they are doing or its effects on a child. They see the other parent to blame for all discord and any emotional problems the child may have. They believe that the special master will see things their way and make rulings accordingly. Parents with the most egregious conduct from the view of an objective observer often see the special master as potentially an ally, as an opportunity to achieve quick justice and vindication at an affordable price. Such individuals usually agree to the appointment of a special master without hesitation.

However, it should be clear from what I have said about the assistance of therapists, attorneys, and special masters in the proof of parental conduct harmful to your child, the more modest the financial resources of the parents, the longer it will take to expose the misconduct to the court — if indeed, it is ever accomplished.

DO'S AND DON'TS

Do . . .

• Let your children know that they are free to have a close and loving relationship with the other parent.

• Have your child evaluated by a child therapist approved by the other parent to determine the need for ongoing therapy even if the child has yet to show symptoms of the stress of your separation.

• If your child is in ongoing counseling with a therapist, seek the agreement (in a writing to be approved by the judge) of the other parent not to call the therapist as a witness in the case.

• Consider enrolling your child in a group counseling program with other children of divorce or separation of about the same age.

• Give the other parent reasonable access to the child and allow the child to call the other parent whenever the child wants to do so. All telephone messages from the other parent should be promptly given to the child and the child should be encouraged to return the call (unless, of course, the other parent has been declared a danger to the child).

• Seek the appointment of a therapist or attorney for the child or of a special master if you are attempting to prove that the other parent is engaged in verbal conduct that will damage your child emotionally.

Don't . . .

• Don't discuss the custody case with your child or seek to obtain from your child a statement of preference for living with you.

• Don't ask your child to keep secrets from the other parent.

• Don't take your child to a therapist for the purpose of finding an expert who will side with you in the custody case. You may wish to seek a second opinion, but this should come only after you have given the neutral court-appointed custody evaluator an opportunity to complete the evaluation and render a recommendation.

• Don't disparage the other parent to the child, even if you sense that the other is disparaging you to your child. If you don't join the game, efforts to alienate your child from you will fail.

• Don't ever expose a child to the verbal or physical abuse of a parent, even when you are the parent who is being abused.

• Don't allow your child to refer to your new mate as "mom" or "dad."

5.

Possible Parenting Plans

The purpose of this brief chapter is to acquaint readers with the possible outcomes of their child custody litigation. As you read other chapters, you may grasp the components of various parenting plans. However, it is important that you understand how some of the jargon of child custody is used and misused so that you will not only fully understand this book, but in order that you will not miscommunicate with others during your custody litigation. It will not be possible to cover all of the terms that have come into vogue in every jurisdiction. For example, it is now fashionable in some jurisdictions not to use the words *custody* or *visitation*, but simply to say each parent will have *contact* or *access* with a child during a given period of time. I applaud elimination of the concept that one parent is a "visitor" with a child. Elimination of the word "custody" or the words "primary custodial parent," however, may make it more difficult for schools and health care providers to know who has the legal right to make certain decisions and where the child's primary residence, if there is one, is located.

Joint Custody/Equal Time-Sharing

Lay people use the words "joint custody" to mean equal time-sharing. This may not be the way that a mental health professional uses these words. To mental health professionals, joint custody may mean any plan where there is "shared parenting," in the sense that both parents are responsible for the well-being of the children for a *significant* period of time. To be "shared" means more than access on alternate weekends and perhaps an overnight during the week without weekend access. In some jurisdictions, the words "joint custody" will be used to describe any plan where both parents have greater than 40 percent access to the children. With such a plan, it is likely that custody is truly shared in that both parents are involved in the children's health care, education, and transportation to various activities. These terms do not have any "correct" meaning. What is important is that you understand that they mean different things to different people. When someone uses the words "joint custody," ask them to explain exactly what they mean, unless it is obvious from the context in which the words were used.

There is one flagrant misuse of the words "joint custody." It is the effort by an evaluator or judge to pacify a noncustodial parent by calling a plan "joint custody" when the noncustodial parent has such limited access to the child that custody is not "joint" or shared in any sense. There was a time when such a ploy could work no mischief, but as I will explain in a later chapter, the right of one parent to relocate to another state with the child can be affected by whether a parenting plan is one of shared or primary custody.

During the late 1980s, equal time-sharing was the fad. Evaluators, having read such books as *Mom's House, Dad's House*, felt that equal time-sharing (or a close approximation thereto) was certainly the best plan for most children. Legislatures were coaxed into making "joint custody" the plan presumed by the judge to be in the children's best interests. Legislators, of course, have the luxury of not having to define their terms, so the public and the courts were left without a clear understanding of what the law meant. While these "presumption" statutes are still the law in many jurisdictions, anyone who works in the field of child custody will tell you that joint custody is no longer the rage. Now it is looked upon with suspicion as a plan that will "confuse" children and expose them to residential instability. There was almost no valid research behind the turn toward joint custody, and there is very little research to support its decline, except in high-conflict cases. Some commentators believe that even the limited research available is hopelessly flawed by the lack of control groups and random samples.

Here's a useful working definition of "joint custody": Over 40 percent of time is spent with each parent. Today, custody evaluators are likely to recommend a joint custody plan in only one or two circumstances. It may be recommended if it is a plan that was already in place at the time of the evaluation and the children seem to be thriving under the plan. But even if such a prior plan is approved for young children, many evaluators will consider the plan too disruptive once a child starts to attend school and needs consistent help with schoolwork. In addition, joint custody may be recommended in cases where (a) the parties were almost equally involved in child care when the parties were together *and* (b) there is relatively little conflict between two good parents who work well together. Neither of these situations comprise even 10 percent of all custody cases that need judicial resolution.

A form of joint custody that was sometimes recommended for a temporary plan during the 1980s is the so-called "nesting arrangement." Under such a plan, the children remain in the family residence and the parents exchange residences every week or so. This was sometimes recommended until both parents had housing that was suitable for overnight stays. One very seldom sees this recommendation anymore; when it is recommended, it is seen as a last resort after all other options have proven untenable for some reason.

The battle over whether joint custody is to be preferred is certainly not a gender-neutral dispute. Because the mother is most often the primary custodial parent, the concept of a primary parent is supported by women's groups all over the country. And because dad is most often the parent to benefit by receiving joint custody (instead of just weekend access), men's groups lobby in their legislatures for joint custody preferences. Unfortunately, children do not have a well-organized and effective group to lobby for them.

The Standard Plan

There is a common parenting plan often called the *standard plan* or *standard access* or *standard visitation* by the noncustodial parent. Indeed, in a few states, if the parents do not agree on a parenting plan, this standard plan, or one approximating it, is automatically ordered without regard to the specific or special needs of the parents or children. This one-size-fits-all approach is judging at its worst and is certainly not in the best interests of children.

The so-called standard plan gives the noncustodial parent contact with the children every other weekend or on two specified weekends per month (e.g., first and third, or second and fourth). While specified weekends reduce the access time of the noncustodial parent for four or so "fifth" weekends per year, the specified approach is preferable if it appears that law enforcement will be called upon to enforce visitation. It is very difficult if not impossible for a police officer to determine who should have the children on a given weekend if the court order merely says "alternating weekends" and each parent claims it is her or his weekend.

The last two weeks of the year are normally divided, with one parent having the children from the day after school is out until Christmas Day, and the other parent having the children from Christmas Day until 6 p.m. on the day before school resumes. Each year the holiday schedule rotates, so that both parents get the period the other parent had the previous year. Thanksgiving is defined as Wednesday after school until the following Sunday at 6 p.m. and is alternated each year. The week of Easter or spring break is also alternated each year, unless there are two one-week breaks from school each year, in which case each parent gets one week. If the noncustodial parent's weekend includes a national Monday holiday, the return of the child is on Monday rather than Sunday.

There are, of course, endless permutations of this standard plan that may fit the needs of the child and parents better than the standard plan. A midweek overnight visit can be scheduled for the week when the parent does not have weekend visitation. Or the noncustodial parent could have a midweek dinner (not overnight) visit every week. The midweek visit has become part of the standard plan in some jurisdictions.

The length of an alternating weekend can be a short Saturday morning to Sunday evening, or a long Friday after school to Monday morning. The typical alternating weekend is from Friday afternoon to Sunday at 6 p.m. A weekend schedule which ends on Monday morning with a return of the children to school, rather than on Sunday evening, is often preferred if the parties live close together and tend to have verbal conflict whenever they are face-to-face.

The Monday morning return to school combined with a Friday after-school pickup prevents any contact between the parents and may help keep the peace.

As is discussed elsewhere, in those states in which the amount of child support is determined in part by the amount of time in which each parent spends with the children, the supported parent may try to deny long weekends and midweek visits for a hidden financial agenda, and the paying parent will seek those visits in order to reduce the amount of child support.

Supervised Visitation

When unsupervised access by one parent will put a child at risk for harm, supervised visitation is the preferred plan. This may be instituted for reasons as benign as that the father has no knowledge of how to care for an infant and needs some parenting classes before he can visit without help. In these cases, a grandmother or an aunt is often an adequate supervisor.

Supervised visitation is clearly indicated when there is misconduct by one parent that threatens a child's safety. The parent may have an alcohol or drug addiction, may be a threat to abduct the child, or may have engaged in spousal or child abuse in the past. The accused parent may be put on supervised visitation as a stopgap protection for the child until the allegations can be investigated. This also occurs when a parent or new mate is accused of molesting the child. Finally, supervised visitation may be the only alternative when one parent is unable or unwilling to cease a continuing campaign of alienation of the children from the other parent.

Suspended Visitation

Family Court judges do not have the authority to permanently terminate one parent's access to a child. This can only be done by the Juvenile Court in dependency proceedings. However, as a last resort or in cases of alleged or proven molestation or abduction, the judge may suspend visitation. The suspension may be for weeks or years, depending upon needs of the children.

In a case of alleged molestation the investigating authorities may not want the parent to have even supervised access to a child until the investigation is concluded or until a criminal trial takes place. In this latter situation, the needs of the prosecutor may be at odds with the child's best interests and the judge must make a difficult call. A child who was physically abused or temporarily abducted may have such great fear of the abusive or abducting parent that even supervised visitation would create painful anxiety in the child. These cases sometimes even call for the termination of telephone contact.

In some cases, an abducted child may be returned having been brainwashed with a totally false belief system about the innocent parent, and the custody evaluator believes that the child needs a time away from the offending parent in order to be able to heal and reconnect with reality.

Suspension of all visitation is always a last resort, and the busiest of judges cannot count five cases in a year in which visitation has been suspended beyond a temporary order pending a hearing within four to six weeks. Supervised visitation is almost always preferred to a suspension of visitation.

DO'S AND DON'TS

Do . . .

• Ask anyone using the term "joint custody" to define it, unless you are absolutely certain of what the person means.

• Determine early on from your attorney if your state or county has a law or policy that favors "joint custody," and if so, what is needed to overcome the presumption.

• Find out how local judges have interpreted the words "joint custody."

• Keep the best interest of your child(ren) foremost. For example, if you suspect that the other parent is attempting to deny you access to the children for financial reasons, consider agreeing not to reduce support based on your expanded visitation. That will allow the other parent to refocus on the children's best interests.

Don't . . .

• Don't expect a Family Court judge ever to *permanently* terminate the other parent's access to a child. It is beyond the judge's authority in all jurisdictions.

• Keep in mind that a parenting plan is always subject to change when circumstances change.

6.

Psychological Evaluations

(This chapter was written by Terry Johnston, Ph.D.,
in collaboration with Judge Stewart)

This chapter is not intended to tell you "how to beat the system" of psychological evaluations. The fact is, you can't. The best thing that you can do for your case is to be truthful. What you will find here are tips to help an adequate parent avoid certain pitfalls that will result in being perceived in an incorrect light. For example, the discussion of punctuality and dress is intended to prevent faux pas. If you are disorganized, insensitive, or ignorant about the importance of the various components of a psychological evaluation, these characteristics will be revealed in one way or the other. The only thing more harmful to your case than possessing these characteristics is to be caught trying to conceal them. To be perceived as devious will destroy your credibility, and seriously hurt your custody case.

How to Approach a Psychological Evaluation

The average person feels quite uneasy when faced with the prospect of being evaluated by a psychologist. It will help to remember two things:

　　• The job of the psychologist is to help work out the best possible parenting plan for your child(ren);

• The psychologist has no "magical powers" and will not be able to read your mind.

Because part of this evaluation may include some amount of feedback to you, try to treat the process as a learning opportunity. Most of us cannot see ourselves as others do, but this is a chance to examine an objective view of yourself, perhaps to obtain some insight into how to avoid sabotaging yourself or repeating failures, and even help you to see valuable aspects of yourself of which you were unaware.

When Is a Complete Psychological Evaluation of the Parents Helpful?

Psychological evaluations with testing are done in only a very small minority of cases. For one thing, these evaluations are expensive — from $800 per parent up to $2,500 at this writing. Very few jurisdictions do testing at county expense, and so a psychological evaluation with testing, like supervised visitation, becomes the prerogative of those who can afford it. Second, a psychological evaluation with testing is not terribly helpful in most cases. If the issue is to determine with which parent a child is more closely bonded, a psychological evaluation will not be helpful. (A process called a *bonding study* may be required, involving a combination of clinical interviews, observations of parent-child interaction, psychological testing, and other assessments of the bond between each child and each parent.)

A fishing expedition, in which the psychological evaluator is asked if the parent has a personality disorder or profile that would affect the person's ability to parent a child, is not likely to be very cost-effective. Many psychologists will try to discourage this type of referral by saying to the judge, "Tell me specifically what you are looking for."

What Are the Limitations of a Psychological Evaluation?

There are many things which a psychological evaluation and testing cannot do. Testing cannot tell the psychologist what the person feels or thinks during the evaluation. Testing cannot conclusively prove a fact, such as "Did he sexually abuse his child?" or Did she lie about her drinking?" Moreover, the psychologist is not trying to learn everything there is to know about the parents. For example, although it is important to know if a parent has sufficient intelligence to function at a minimum level in our culture, the parent's I.Q. is probably irrelevant to a custody case and such tests will not be performed. It is probably not relevant to a custody case to obtain a complete diagnostic picture, as might be required in a hospital or other clinical setting.

The psychologist performing the psychological evaluation virtually never makes custody or treatment recommendations, although some very obvious suggestions may be offered. The psychologist may suggest a referral for a medical or psychiatric evaluation if it appears that there are some problem behaviors which may be related to physical illness or neurological processes.

Who Gets Evaluated?

It is unlikely that a custody evaluator or a judge will ask for a psychological evaluation of one party alone. The issues in family court involve parenting, and thus the judge or custody evaluator will want both parties to be tested and evaluated. An evaluation of both parents will often tell the judge more about the dynamics of their relationship, and that can be valuable information.

Once in a great while, however, there may be a request for the evaluation of only one parent. Such a request might be made in a case where the parent has a history of hospitalization for depression or suicidal behavior; the judge or custody evaluator needs to know that the problem no longer interferes with the parent's functioning. An observation by the custody evaluator of bizarre behavior or the discovery that one parent has had a period of amnesia could lead to a request to evaluate only one of the parents.

When Does the Evaluation Begin?

The psychologist's observations will probably start when you first speak by telephone to set up appointments. Are you polite and cooperative? Does the evaluation process have a priority in your life (as indicated by how difficult it is to schedule the time)? Are you curt or suspicious during this first contact? Do you begin to inappropriately try to tell "your" story? Do you express anger at the other parent even before you meet the psychologist? Are you on time for the interviews? Did you have to call back several times to check on the time? Did you give the psychologist your complete attention or did you take four phone calls on your cell phone during the first hour of the interview? Capable but busy parents can make any of these mistakes. Don't let that parent be you.

There are a few obvious rules to follow if you are ordered to submit to a psychological examination. Be courteous and succinct on the telephone. Punctuality and appearance are even more important in this setting than the meeting with the custody evaluator. Judges find that virtually every report on the results of a psychological evaluation with testing starts out with a comment on how quickly the appointment was made, how punctual the parent was in arriving at the interview, and whether or not the subject was appropriately dressed. That should tell you how important these factors can be. Tardiness, missed appointments, and cancellations will often be perceived as a lack of cooperativeness or organization, even though you are normally cooperative and well organized.

When a psychologist says that a parent was "dressed appropriately," this is likely to mean that the person dressed within the broad range of ordinary, and with some recognition of the seriousness of the process. Casual clothes are perfectly acceptable; shorts, sandals, tank tops and T-shirts are not. Such dress conveys the impression that the parent is treating the process in an overly casual way. The mechanic who apologizes for arriving in work clothes is dressed appropriately. The pinstripe-suited attorney is probably appropriate. A pinstriped suit on a mechanic may raise some questions about the meaning of the costume. The barefooted woman in an ankle-length dress, the mother in a glamorous cocktail dress, or the woman whose outfit resembles Judy Garland's in *The Wizard of Oz* communicates messages to the psychologist to be on the lookout for other unusual aspects of the parent's behavior. Of course, the psychologist will be on the lookout for such negative behaviors as nodding off or smelling of alcohol.

How Should You Act During a Psychological Evaluation?

The most important part of a psychological evaluation is the expert opinion of the psychologist assigned by the court. Psychological testing may be one element of the evaluation, to provide an objective confirmation of the psychologist's clinical observations during the interview(s). For example, the psychologist may sense that a parent is particularly fearful, and the parent's test profile may show high anxiety and paranoia scores; the testing has verified a clinical observation. The psychologist will then explore further the basis of the parent's fears and the credibility of that parent's reports. In order to arrive at an opinion of the parent's emotional makeup, the psychologist may have to do some investigation to determine how truthful or credible the person is being in the interviews. Keep in mind that the observations are the most important part of the psychological evaluation.

The psychologist will probably want to know your view of the custody conflict, and what you are hoping the outcome of the court process will be. In order to know who you are as a parent, a psychologist will want to know something of your history. It is very helpful if you have given this some thought so that when you are asked to talk about who you are, where you came from, and what your relationship with your parents and siblings was like when you were small, you can discuss these matters coherently and save time for everyone. In addition, the psychologist will probably want you to describe your past relationship with any former partners. Of great importance is how you describe your child or children, how you see that relationship as having been changed by the separation, and what you might be able to do to improve the relationship.

Do not fail to refer to people in your life by name. If you refer only to "my ex," "my boss," "my son," "the girl," etc., the evaluator may conclude that you don't think of these people as unique individuals, but you view them by their roles in your life.

If you reveal a high level of anger, the psychologist will suspect that you have impulse-control problems, unless you can convince the psychologist that your anger is controlled, does not result in inappropriate conduct, and is justified under the circumstances. That is a huge task. It is better just not to become inappropriately angry (although I think most psychologists would agree that true anger cannot, and should not, be concealed during the evaluation process).

You must demonstrate that you are a person in control of your thoughts and mental processes from the moment of the first contact with the process of psychological evaluation. Answer questions asked as completely as you can, but do not wander off on tangents or appear to be wanting to tell "your" story. Respond to what the psychologist wants to know about you, your background, and your relationship to the other parent and the children. Long rambling answers or responses that are irrelevant to the question asked will always be mentioned in the psychologist's report to the judge or custody evaluator, and will generally be said to be indicative of a flawed thought process or some other disorder.

Do not try to be someone other than who you are. You can't do that successfully, and moreover it would not be in the best interests of your children if you could. Keep in mind that for the other parent to test out as "perfect" is so rare that it will not happen.

The advice in chapter 2 — to phrase any criticism of the other parent as conduct that "concerns" you because of its effect on the children — is just as applicable when undergoing a psychological evaluation.

If there are allegations of domestic violence, abuse, or alienation, the psychologist will want to explore those questions. It is important to gather any available factual evidence, such as restraining orders, police reports, probation reports, or alcoholism or drug testing results.

Most psychologists will take notes during the interview process, although a few prefer to tape record. You will be informed of any recording, since it is unethical to tape an interview surreptitiously, and the evaluation could thus be excluded from evidence. Should you attempt to record secretly, you will make a very bad impression!

A good clinician is a very acute observer, and is able to add together all of the tiny aspects of appearance, history, test results, and behavior to come to a description of the parents which explains the current situation.

What Psychological Testing Will Likely Be Required?

Psychological evaluations may involve some form of psychological testing. The psychologist will decide — based on the court's order — what kind of testing should be done, if any. (In the jurisdictions of which I am aware, only licensed psychologists — Ph.D., Ed.D., or Psy.D. — are recognized by the court as qualified to administer tests.)

It is most likely that you will be asked, in the first interview or earlier, to complete one or more rather long paper-and-pencil questionnaires which will ask you questions about your preferences and beliefs. One of the most commonly used tests is the *Minnesota Multiphasic Personality Inventory II* (MMPI-2). Another is the *Millon Clinical Multiaxial Inventory-3* (MCMI-3). These tests have been administered to hundreds of thousands of persons all over the country. With computer scoring and analysis, your answers will be compared with those of persons from all walks of life with all kinds of personality characteristics and emotional makeups, generating a personality profile that describes you.

Some of the questions will address your psychological state at the time you take the test. The psychologist understands that there will be differences between your emotional state when you are experiencing the stress of a high-conflict custody battle and your more usual emotional state. Some questions will address more stable traits and behaviors that make up your personality. These results should be fairly consistent over time.

Although some of the questions may seem irrelevant or repetitive, it is important that you answer all of them without agonizing over the answers. Most people take an hour or two to complete the MMPI; if you take five hours and omit fifty questions, you will be sufficiently out of the ordinary that the psychologist will wonder why. Are you highly suspicious, extraordinarily indecisive, unable to remain in contact with the task at hand, or deliberately misleading?

Another type of test sometimes selected for custody psychological evaluations is known as a "projective" test. These devices ask you to respond to an ambiguous image — a drawing, an irregular shape, an ink blot — so that the psychologist may interpret your response and thereby reflect your own thoughts, ideas, values, and personality. Common examples of widely used projective tests are the *Rorschach Test* and the *Thematic Apperception Test*.

Ideally, the psychologist will choose questionnaires or tests that assess your present state of mind, your lifestyle, your perceptions about your children and your relationship with them. You may be asked to do some drawings similar to those your children may be asked to produce if they are subject to a psychological evaluation or if they meet with the custody evaluator. This can help the evaluator see the difference in how each member of the family views each other and the family system.

Can You "Beat" the Tests?

The MMPI and MCMI have scales built into them that will measure how important it is to you to look very good, or to look sick or pathetic. The examiner and the court know that you want to "look good," because the test is administered in the context of custody litigation. However, if you maintain that you have never told an untruth in your entire life, your answer is not believable and it shows that you are making a conscious effort to answer the questions in a way that will put you in a favorable light, rather than answering the questions truthfully. Psychologists call this "faking good." An experienced psychologist knowledgeable about custody disputes will expect some effort to present yourself in a favorable light, but if your answers are well outside the average in "faking good," the results will be suspect.

Anyone who cares enough to take some care with their appearance has certain narcissistic traits that most of us have, but it is something else to have a "narcissistic personality disorder," with little ability to respond to the needs of those around you. Similarly, it is one thing to feel a little less guilt than others do, and to be an especially good salesperson; it is another to have an "antisocial personality disorder," hurting others without concern because you have little or no empathy for other people. Answer all questions truthfully! "Faking good" will be detected. Moreover persons faking good seldom have great insight into their own behavior.

Confidentiality

Ordinarily, when a psychologist sees a client for psychotherapy, the communications of the client are privileged and the client "holds the privilege." This means that everything that is said or any conclusions the psychologist reaches must be kept confidential unless the client waives the privilege. (There are certain exceptions in the law for cases of danger to self or others.) However, parents, children, or a family being seen under court order for a psychological or custody evaluation are *not* the clients or patients of the therapist, and they have no privilege or right of confidentiality. The judge, special master, or other officer of the court who orders the evaluation "holds the privilege."

For example, Judge Brown may send the Smiths to Dr. White for a custody or psychological evaluation. The results of the evaluation will be summarized in a report that Dr. White sends to Judge Brown or the court officer she designates. If the evaluation was a psychological evaluation, the results will be sent to the custody evaluator. If a custody evaluation was done, the results will be sent to the attorneys and the court. It will thereby be available to the judge at the time of trial. The judge or the special master or the evaluator is going to use the information in the report as one of the pieces of information on which the decision will be based. If the report is from a custody evaluator, the report may indeed be the most important piece of information in the case.

However, although the report will be released to the referring party, and although each party may have access to the information presented to the evaluator by the other party, the therapist doing the custody or psychological evaluation is not permitted to reveal information about either parent or the family to anyone outside the court system.

If the case is a highly conflicted one and the judge has appointed an attorney or a guardian for the litigation to represent the children's best interests, that guardian or attorney has the right to see the report. In all jurisdictions, at some point the parties and their attorneys will have the right to see all reports that any witness will rely on and even the notes of the evaluator. In the case of a psychological evaluation, the attorneys and the parents will be able to obtain the raw test data. They can have this material and the evaluator's report reviewed by another expert to see if the findings follow logically from the raw data, and if the recommendations in the report follow logically from the findings. This second psychological expert will be available to testify at trial, but may not be called to testify unless his findings differ from those of the court-appointed expert.

The ethical standards of the American Psychological Association — and most, if not all, state psychological associations — require that the raw data and results of a psychological examination be delivered to a parent's expert rather than to the attorney or parent directly. The expert is normally a psychologist professionally trained and licensed to review and interpret the data and the report. However, state law may come into conflict with the association's rules and the data and report may be given to an attorney or parent who is without training to interpret the data, the findings, or the report.

If the report of the psychological evaluator is entered into evidence at trial, it becomes part of the public record and is open to inspection by anyone who might care to review the report, including the children when they are older. However, this is very rare. Although litigants often lose sleep over who will look at their court files and record, the fact is that usually no one cares enough to spend the time. The greatest abuse of reports by custody and psychological evaluators is committed by the parents themselves. Parents with poor judgment and skewed boundaries may attempt to read to the children information critical of the other parent, or to disseminate the information to teachers or relatives. The former is certainly child abuse.

What About Testing the Children?

When a psychologist interviews and observes children or tests them, either for a custody or psychological evaluation, it is especially important for the therapist to respect the child's privacy. The therapist should explain to the child in very carefully selected, age-appropriate language that the child will not be asked to make decisions or express a preference about which parent the child will live with primarily, or to report negative things about either parent. On the other hand, an experienced evaluator should be able to obtain from the child and describe in a report a child's situation, the child's needs, and the child's perceptions without quoting the child or impairing that child's relationship with either parent.

Parents can help to make the evaluative process a less threatening one for their children by describing to them that they are going to meet with a person whose job it is to help all of them and the judge in making a parenting plan. It may help to explain to a young child that this is a "doctor for talking about feelings," not a doctor that gives shots or pills when the child is sick. The child should be told that this is not a doctor that takes sides, but really wants to get to know everyone in the family, and to help all in the family to figure out ways of the children sharing their parents that could be better for everyone.

Suppose a Psychological Evaluator Concludes That You Have a Personality Disorder?

One reason that you need a local attorney experienced in custody litigation is that such an attorney should have a store of knowledge that can be of help to you if the result of your psychological evaluation is less than flattering to you. Your attorney will know that some psychological testing is highly controversial and there is a respectable body of opinion that believes that some of the testing is worthless as a measure of a person's ability to be a good parent.

(However, the correlation would seem to be quite logical to most people, including your judge.) Your attorney should know that in most jurisdictions the judge cannot even use a personality disorder in arriving at a decision unless there is some evidence that the disorder will significantly affect your ability to parent a child.

Your attorney will also know that there are tests and there are tests. While many psychologists believe that the MMPI and the MCMI are helpful tools in evaluating a person's personality structure and parenting ability, a number of respected academic (research) and clinical psychologists have misgivings about the use of the Rorschach and certain other projective tests described earlier, as well as the *House-Tree-Person,* or *sentence completion* exercises in evaluations of parents and children. Indeed, a psychologist who bases conclusions about parenting abilities on the images a parent sees in Rorschach ink blots may well look absolutely ridiculous under cross-examination by a knowledgeable attorney.

Your attorney will know that the MMPI and the MCMI are usually scored by a computer, and that the basis for the conclusion that certain answers you have given reveal a certain personality profile or disorder is that, in the past, persons with such disorders answered the questions in the way that you have answered them. Thus your attorney may dispute a claim that every person who answers questions in a given way has a certain personality disorder or profile.

Your attorney also knows that it is your right to see the results of your psychological evaluation and that of the other parent a reasonable time prior to a hearing in which the evaluations will be part of the evidence. Many psychologists and custody evaluators are reluctant to allow the parent to see the result of the other parent's test. They believe that the results will be divisive and make settlement more difficult. While the reports may be withheld from you and your attorney early on in the case, your attorney knows that you cannot be required to settle the case or go to a custody hearing without access to the reports. They are relevant evidence. Indeed, for an attorney to settle a custody case without seeing the report on each parent should make the attorney's insurance carrier nervous. You and your attorney absolutely must see and copy both reports, as well as the raw test data, if you intend to ask your own privately retained psychologist to evaluate the work done by the person appointed by the judge or the custody evaluator who evaluates you and the other parent. Without that information, there is no way to evaluate the work done prior to a hearing or trial on custody in which the test results will be part of the evidence.

An experienced family law attorney will know the importance of demanding the raw test data for any test that will be used to question your ability as a parent. For example, your attorney knows that any pattern of answers to the MMPI will reveal both positive and negative personality characteristics. If the evaluator has concentrated only on one or the other as contained in the test report, she should be questioned about the basis for selecting only flattering or only unflattering characteristics. An experienced attorney will also want another expert to look at the raw test data on the other parent to see if the selectivity of the psychologist favored one parent over the other. However, your attorney knows that it is legitimate for the psychologist to be attentive to those profiles which support the psychologist's clinical observations and to ignore those that are irrelevant to the clinical observations. The psychologist is, after all, evaluating the person who has been interviewed and has seemed to reveal certain characteristics, not a total stranger.

Moreover, a local attorney experienced in custody cases should know how much weight the judges to whom your case may be assigned give to psychological evidence of a person's personality structure. Some judges find such information to be quite helpful in reaching a decision; others look at it as one would look upon a form of voodoo, and view all mental health professionals with suspicion. Indeed, some judges, in various parts of the country, doubt the value of psychologists and psychotherapy altogether. Many parents believe that the psychologist will consider them to be "crazy." This is absurd. Every human being is unique, and deviates in some ways from the statistical "norm." Only the most significant personality disorders are likely to be an important factor in custody decisions.

It's worth keeping in mind a common joke among psychologists: all trial attorneys would test out as far more "narcissistic" or "obsessive-compulsive" than the average person!

DO'S AND DON'TS

Do ...

• If ordered to a psychological evaluation, be prompt and appropriately dressed.

• Maintain a calm, thoughtful, and confident demeanor throughout the interview portion of the evaluation.

• In the interview, be sure you answer the question that is asked, and then stop.

• If the report on your psychological profile is harmful to your case, and if you can afford it, pay for your attorney to have the raw test data and the conclusions of the psychologist evaluated by your own privately retained expert psychologist.

• Have your attorney obtain a copy of the evaluator's report on each parent well in advance of any custody hearing and before you are asked to settle the case. It is your right to see any document a judge might rely upon in reaching a decision.

• If you can afford it, retain an attorney with sufficient experience to know how much weight psychological evidence carries with each judge to whom your case may be assigned.

• Realize that in the process of a psychological evaluation you are under scrutiny from the first phone call you make to set up an appointment.

• Understand that clinical observations of you by the psychologist are of greater importance in the ultimate result than the psychological tests you may be given.

• Before your first meeting with the psychologist, try to give some thought to who you are, where you came from, and your relationship with your parents and siblings, if any.

Don't . . .

• During the interview portion of the psychological evaluation, don't gratuitously focus on the difficulties and unhappiness of your childhood or the problems within the family in which you grew up.

• In your interviews with the psychologist, don't take calls on your cell phone or focus undue attention on your watch.

• Don't try to answer written tests in a way that will make it appear that you are without faults. Don't "fake good."

• Don't let anger control your responses to interview questions.

• In the interview, don't try to tell "your" story rather than responding to the specific questions asked of you.

• Don't believe that you must either settle your case or go to a custody hearing without seeing the evaluator's report on each parent.

• Don't forget that some psychological testing is highly controversial and a body of respected academic and clinical psychologists doubt that "projective" testing (in contrast with the MMPI and the MCMI) is of any value whatever in evaluating a person's ability as a parent.

• Don't worry about public scrutiny of your divorce file or the public record of your case. Unless you are a very big celebrity, no one beyond those involved really cares about your divorce or custody dispute.

7.

Relocation Cases

The Custodial Parent Can Move Away With the Children

Prior to 1991, most family court judges throughout the United States assumed that the primary custodial parent could move with a child any place in the world that the parent wanted to go and the noncustodial parent could not prevent the move unless it could be shown that the move would be detrimental to the child. In custody law, a showing of detriment imposes a burden of proof that can be met only in a very unusual case. The move could not be blocked by showing that it was not in a child's best interests. The move, to be prevented, would have to have some direct and untoward consequence on the child. For example, a move to an area where the climate would cause an allergic or asthmatic child to be continually ill, or to a part of the world where competent medical care was not available for a child.

A 180-Degree Change in the Law

In 1991, a California appellate court rendered its decision in *In Re Marriage of Carlson,* saying that the assumption that had been made by so many courts — that the custodial parent was free to relocate a child wherever that parent wished — was *wrong*. Indeed, *Carlson* said that the test was not one of *detriment* as previously thought, but of *the best interests of the child*. A custodial parent who wished to move to an area where the other parent did not reside would have to show that the move was in the best interests of the child. In determining best interests, the trial judge was to balance the interest of the child in remaining near the other parent — so the child could have frequent and continual contact with both parents — against the interest of the child in living with the custodial parent in an area remote from the other parent.

The *Carlson* case was a statement that a child gets stability from two parents active in the child's life, and an affirmation that the policy of the State of California was to give a child frequent and continuing contact with both parents. Moreover, the parent wishing to relocate with the child had to prove that the move was a necessity, not merely convenient. In addition, the parent was required to establish that the move was not motivated by a desire to deprive the other parent of contact with the child. As you might guess, California judges began to deny relocation requests in a large number of cases. Only where the other parent's role in the child's life was minimal or had been inappropriate was a move approved.

Keep in mind that while lawyers and judges may talk in terms of a ruling that held that mom or dad could not move, this is a shorthand way of saying that the parent cannot move *the child*. A parent has a constitutional right to live anywhere the parent desires. A court can only restrain the move of a *child*, and only then when the parents are living apart and are in litigation over paternity or in a dissolution or separation litigation.

A short time later, in 1992, another California Appellate District rendered a decision in *In re Marriage of McGinnis*. That case set forth the procedural rules for relocation cases. *McGinnis* held that the first duty of the judge in a move-away case was to restrain the move until a full and complete investigation (evaluation) could be done and a full and complete hearing held on the best interests of the children. The trial judge in *McGinnis* was reversed for permitting the move before the required full investigation, report, and hearing. Some trial judges, including your author, believe that the trial judge, even after *McGinnis*, can permit an interim move of the child in an appropriate case while the evaluation is proceeding.

. . . And Back Again — The Current Law

Five years after *Carlson*, the California Supreme Court — in a 1996 decision of national significance — voiced its disapproval of the entire line of cases starting with *Carlson* as it reversed the Court of Appeal for denying the move (*In re Marriage of Burgess*). The state Supreme Court said that a custodial parent need not show that the move is a necessity, and that the proper test is *not* "the best interests of the children." Rather, the parent objecting to the move must show that the move is such a detriment to the child that an immediate change of custody is required to protect the health and welfare of the child.

To make such a showing is extremely difficult. It is generally thought that this burden of proof can be met only in cases where teenage children are objecting to being removed from their school and their friends, in cases where a move would have a direct effect on a child's health, and perhaps in a very few other instances. The only thing required of the parent wishing to move is that the move not be in bad faith, i.e. designed to deny the other parent frequent contact with the child. As you surely suspect, thousands of parents who would have been restrained under the old *Carlson* line of cases are now able to move. *Burgess* appears to be a rejection of the notion that a child obtains stability from having two active parents, and a statement that the child obtains stability from the primary custodial parent and the bond with that parent is not to be easily broken by a court.

Carlson and *Burgess* are certainly not gender-neutral. The mother is more often the custodial parent and is thus more often the parent wishing to move. Women's groups were hostile to the *Carlson* line of cases and greeted *Burgess* with great cheer. Men's groups, feeling that *Burgess* marginalized their importance in the lives of their children, were unhappy — if not outraged — at *Burgess*. In most cases, the father's only chance to prevent a move is to convince an evaluator that mom's motives should be suspect. This will likely be a successful strategy only where the reason for the move is very flimsy, or where prior to the move the mother has established a record of interfering with the father's access to the child and unreasonably attempting to block the father's frequent contact with the child.

What If One Parent Under a Joint Custody Plan Wants to Relocate With the Children?

Burgess did not give trial courts much guidance in how to deal with a move-away case wherein one parent in a shared or joint custody plan seeks to relocate the child away from the home of the other parent. This issue was touched upon only in a footnote, in which the court stated that in cases of joint custody a "best-interests" test should be applied. Unfortunately, very little guidance to lower courts can be given in a footnote. What did the court mean by "joint custody"? An equal time share? Does the label of joint custody determine the legal test to be applied regardless of what the actual sharing of time with the child may be? Suppose the time-share percentage is 60–40; is that "joint custody" as the court used the words?

Most trial judges have concluded that the court did not mean that the label of joint custody or primary custody would be decisive, but that each case needs to be carefully reviewed to see if the parents have a shared parenting plan or a plan in which there is a primary custodial parent. As noted in chapter 2, I consider a parenting plan in which each parent has the child over 40 percent of the time to be joint custody, and a plan where one parent has more than 60 percent to represent primary custody. The difficult cases, in which the extent of each parent's involvement in the children's lives must be scrutinized, are those where one parent's time falls between 39 percent and 42 percent.

In two recent cases, the Courts of Appeal apparently adopted a lower percentage standard. The courts held that in one case 36%, and in another 38%, was not significant time with a child and thus constituted primary custody by the other parent. I have followed Santa Clara County's rules for determining percentages, which are consistent with those propounded by the *California Family Law Report* published by Steve Adams. The Courts of Appeal may have used a different method in concluding that the percentages should be lower.

Moreover, the footnote in *Burgess* gives no indication of the factors to be balanced in a best-interests test. Are we to go back to *Carlson*, wherein the court is to determine whether it is in the child's best interests to be in one area with both parents, as opposed to being with the custodial parent in an area remote from the other parent? That is probably not the proper test, since *Burgess* so clearly rejects the notion that frequent and continuing contact with both parents is the source of a child's stability. It is more likely that the California Supreme Court, in a "joint custody" case, would approve a hearing that determines again (as may have already been determined if a trial was held when joint custody was instituted) which parent is the inherently better caretaker.

This time around, however, the court cannot find parents so equal that a joint custody plan is found to be proper. Joint custody is not an option where the parents do not live in the same geographical area. In such cases, the trial judge must pick a primary custodial parent. Unfortunately, no one knows for sure what form of balancing test the California Supreme Court — or a trial, appellate, or supreme court in another state — would approve for relocation cases involving joint custody.

(It is of interest to note that I have kept track of the many cases in which I have felt compelled to approve a move-away request under the rule of *Burgess*, and in every case the evaluator has said that under the *Carlson* test of best interests, the relocation of the child that I have approved has been contrary to the best interests of the child.)

Many California judges felt that the legislature might step in and establish a rule for relocation cases by statute. One retired Court of Appeal justice with a marvelous sense of humor suggested that the legislature would surely act to overrule *Burgess*. The law requires California legislators to live in California, so only their ex-spouses could request to move out of state with their children. Surely, he reasoned, the lawmakers would put a stop to that! However, thus far the legislature has failed to act. It may be that opposing pressures from men's and women's groups are so intense that the politicians believe it is better to do nothing.

Most judges also have taken the view that despite the *Burgess* decision, *McGinnis* is still the law in California, in that the relocation of the child cannot be approved without a complete investigation or evaluation and a full hearing (if one is requested by the noncustodial parent). As noted earlier, many judges believe that *McGinnis* allows a judge to approve or deny an interim move pending completion of the evaluation and hearing. Judges are unlikely to approve an interim move unless it appears certain that the final order will not return the child to California.

The Effect of *Burgess* on Child Custody Litigation

The *Burgess* decision has caused fewer child custody cases to settle without a trial. Dads are now far more reluctant to agree to parenting plans in which moms are the primary custodial parent because the dads fear that their children may be taken across the country within a year or so. Dads feel that if they can obtain a shared parenting plan, then under a best-interests test, they may be able to block a relocation of their children. On the other hand, relocation cases where an interim move has been approved are now far less likely to go to a trial after the evaluation; dad could see the handwriting on the wall when the interim move was approved. The judge would not have approved an *interim* move unless it was likely that the *final* order after an evaluation would also approve the move.

The Effect of *Burgess* on Other States

Many family law judges nationwide hold the view that changes in the law often "start in California and move east." That would appear to be true in relocation cases. While the *Carlson* versus *Burgess* approaches were being fought out in California, most states had little published law on the subject of relocation cases. The extent to which other state courts followed *Carlson* before *Burgess* overruled *Carlson* is very hard to determine. However, as best I can tell, most trial judges in other states have opted to follow the *Burgess* case rather than *Carlson*, if for no other reason than it is the opinion of a higher court. State trial court decisions are normally not published as Appellate Court opinions are, and thus there is still not a great deal of published case law on relocation cases in other states.

It is my prediction that, as time passes and relocation cases reach the appellate level, the great majority of the states — if not all — will fall in line behind *Burgess*. As a result, the idea that it is of the greatest importance that a child have two active parents will be diminished nationwide, at least in the courts. Critics of *Burgess* see it as a return to the old "tender years" doctrine, at least as far as move-away cases are concerned. Under that doctrine, custody of children of "tender years" was presumed to be awarded to the mother unless she was found to be "unfit."

Burgess also tells us that the trial court, at the time a move of the children is approved, can provide for the most expanded visitation possible by the noncustodial parent, and can require the moving parent to pay all of the costs of transportation. This will be of benefit to the parent left behind unless the financial circumstances are such that the parties will not be able to pay for the children to travel. In cases where the parents have no resources to pay for travel, the noncustodial parent — most often dad — has truly lost his children.

Do Not Relocate Your Children Without the Permission of a Court or the Written Permission of the Other Parent

If you reside in a state where *Burgess* has been or is likely to be adopted by the courts, and you move your children away without the consent of the court or the written consent of the other parent, you are asking for legal difficulties. The other parent — again, most often dad — will file a paternity or dissolution action and allege that the children have been abducted or moved without his consent. The judge will likely order the children immediately returned to the home state, and they will remain there until a hearing on an interim move can be held or a full evaluation is completed. Your life and the lives of your children will be disrupted and the expense will be enormous. Moreover, if your unilateral move is seen as an abduction of the children that ignores the rights of the other parent and is thus an act inconsistent with good parenting, you could lose whatever custodial rights you had before you moved the child. The consent of the other parent *must* be in writing. In a large number of cases the parent alleged to have given consent "a month ago" denies ever having done so.

Even if you or the children are the victims of abuse, it is still better that you not leave the state if possible. When the other parent goes to court to obtain an order for the children to be returned, no one will be present to explain that you left because of abuse. And even if an attorney should be able to represent you after you leave, the judge may either not believe the allegation or decide that the children should be returned until the truth can be investigated. There are women's shelters in virtually every community in which you and the children can reside until you can get a judge to approve an interim move. These shelters can give you excellent practical — and often legal — advice. While not a highly desirable living arrangement, they are certainly better for you and the children than living with an abusive spouse.

There are some situations in which the abused parent (usually, but not always, mom) will feel compelled to seek the support and shelter of her family in another state. If so, the fleeing parent should try to get word of her plight to those officials who will be involved in the decision on the custody of the children and her ultimate right to move. Some states have statutes permitting an abused mother to inform the county prosecutor, district attorney, or whoever would have the duty of seeking to locate an abducted child, that she is fleeing the state because of physical abuse to her or the children. The authority so advised will then refuse to seek the return of the children to the home state or even to locate the children. In addition, the authority will inform the judge whose assistance the abuser is seeking that the mother left the state because of abuse.

Even if there is no such notification provision in the statutes of your home state, you may be able to hire an attorney who will personally alert any judge the abuser might approach for help of the true facts of why you fled the state. (Such notification is not difficult because, even in large metropolitan areas, there are only a few judges to whom the abuser's request for a return of the children would be directed.)

DO'S AND DON'TS

Do . . .

• If you wish to relocate with your child, ask a family law attorney whether your state is one that has followed *Burgess* in published opinions or, if not, whether your trial judge is apt to do so. Prior to any move, obtain a clear understanding of the status of the law in your jurisdiction.

• If the other parent seeks to relocate your children without reasonable notice to you in advance, insist on a full evaluation and hearing on the issue, and oppose any effort for an interim move of your children pending that hearing.

• If, at the time the issue of custody first arises, you have any doubts about the other parent's desire to remain in the area where you reside, seek a parenting plan in which you have the children in your custody at least 40 percent of the time, and insist that it be described as a "joint custody" plan.

• If you or the children are the victims of abuse and you must leave the state for your protection or for financial or other reasons, make every effort to notify the authorities — and any judge from whom the abuser might seek an order for the children to be returned to the home state — of the fact that you are leaving because of fear for your safety and/or that of your children.

• Accept the fact that if the judge has approved an interim move of the other parent and your children to another state or a location some distance from your home, the judge is likely to give final approval to the move at a hearing held after a full evaluation of the issue. If an interim move is approved, seek the broadest possible visitation rights during the interim period. Focus in settlement discussions on expanding or maintaining these rights and seeking an agreement that the relocating parent pay the majority if not all of transportation expenses for the children.

• Beware of the advice of any attorney who tells you that you are free to leave the state with the children simply because there is, as yet, no order from any court restraining a move of the children.

Don't ...

• If you fear that the other parent may try to relocate your children to an area remote from your home, don't agree to a parenting plan where the other parent is labeled as the primary custodial parent.

• Don't ever attempt to relocate with a child without the permission of the court or the written permission of the other parent.

• If at all possible, don't leave the state with your children, even if you or the children are the victims of physical abuse.

• If you wish to relocate with your children, don't retain an attorney who cannot give you a clear description of the current law of relocation in your jurisdiction, and, if the law is uncertain, the inclination of your local judges to follow decisions in other states, such as California's *Burgess* decision.

• Don't agree that the primary custodial parent can relocate with your children if the primary parent's past efforts to block your access to the children will cause the custody evaluator to suspect that the motive for the move is to deny you frequent access to your children.

8.

Child Abuse and False Accusations of Molestation

What is child abuse? The answer will depend upon the attitudes of the community and the judge who hears your case. Judges normally reflect, to some extent, the attitudes and values of the jurisdiction in which they sit. What may be child abuse in a large metropolitan area or in a highly educated community may not be classified as child abuse in rural areas or in suburban areas of low education and income. What is appropriate in regard to a child also differs along religious and ethnic lines.

There are some *physical acts* that almost any judge would find to be child abuse:

- locking a child in a closet
- depriving a child of food for a substantial period of time
- slaps across the face
- blows to the head with a fist
- strikes with a solid object
- a burn
- kicking a child
- beating a child with a belt
- "washing a child's mouth out" with soap
- any form of sexual misconduct with a child, even if the child is

fully clothed at the time and the misconduct occurs only once and for only a few seconds. Sexual harassment of a preteen or teenager is sexual abuse.

Physical violence is certainly not the only form of abuse. Most mental health professionals would consider the following to be psychological child abuse:

• acts of domestic violence committed in the presence of a child
• efforts to alienate a child from the other parent
• disparaging the other parent in the presence of the child
• enmeshing a child in the litigation by discussing it with the child
• attempting to align the child with one parent's point of view
• taking a child to multiple therapists in an effort to find an ally for the litigation.

It is certainly not abuse to tell a child to take a "time out" and go to his or her room for a time. Most judges would allow an occasional hand to the rear end, so long as it is done with measured restraint, but there are many mental health professionals who consider such a blow — indeed, *any* striking of a child — to be abusive. Almost no verbal reprimand will be considered by the court to be abuse, even those that do emotional harm such as words that suggest that the child has not merely done wrong but is inherently a bad person.

There are a series of acts that fall into a gray area and one cannot be certain whether the court or evaluator will find such conduct abusive. Suppose the hand to the backside leaves a red mark or hand print? What about a cold shower on a cold day? That is indeed a painful experience to some children. Suppose the child is ordered to his/her room for six or more hours? Is it child abuse to forcibly shake a child who is over 6 years of age? Of course no good parent would recommend these forms of punishment, but are they child abuse?

What Constitutes Neglect of a Child?

Acts of *neglect* commonly seen by judges and custody evaluators include:
• failure to provide food for a child
• leaving a young child alone for an extended period of time
• failure to meet a child's medical and dental needs
• leaving a young child locked in a car

- failure to change an infant's diapers causing rashes and sores
- use of unqualified sitters and day care providers
- failure to protect a child from an abusive mate.

Acts that are detrimental to a child but probably not neglect that will bring court intervention would be the failure to take the child for dental and physical checkups, failure to see that a child has all necessary immunization shots, or the failure to treat head lice or a flea infestation and to do whatever fumigation of the home that may be necessary to prevent their return.

What If the Judge Concludes That a Child Is Being Abused?

What a judge will do when a child is being abused depends upon the facts of the particular case. Of course a judge could place primary custody of a child with the other parent. If the abuser was not the primary custodian, the abuser's access could be suspended or limited to supervised visits. The offending parent can be ordered into parenting classes or anger management instruction or both. The facts of any case limit what a family court judge can do. In most jurisdictions, a family court judge has no authority to place a child into foster care or a group home at public expense. That power is reserved to a juvenile court judge. The family court judge can only ask the juvenile court to look at a case to see if the latter believes the situation is grave enough that the juvenile court should take jurisdiction.

The judge is limited in what can be done by a number of factors. The parenting abilities or availability of the other parent must be considered. The extent to which the child is bonded to the abusive parent (and may not really know the other parent) must be weighed. The financial circumstances of the parties will certainly be a factor if the judge wishes to consider visitation monitored by a professional supervisor.

Whatever a judge decides to do, the first step is to be certain that the allegation of abuse has been substantiated. Allegations of abuse, like those of alcohol and drug use, can be used by parents in a custody battle as a ploy to gain advantage. The judge must be certain of the truth of the charge before taking any action that will affect a child in the long term. Of course the judge may make a temporary placement of a child pending a complete investigation of the charges. Such a placement is normally considered to be "without prejudice," i.e., it will not establish a *status quo* that will influence a later custody award if the charges are not substantiated.

The Molestation Charge

Child molestation is frequently alleged to obtain an advantage in a custody dispute. The allegation almost invariably made against the father by the mother, or by the father against the mother's new mate. Only occasionally is it made against another family member.

The allegation of molestation is ripe for misuse and abuse because, unlike the allegation of substance abuse, it is very difficult to prove or disprove. It is an act that is always committed in private. There are no witnesses to corroborate or refute the allegation. In many instances, the truth or falsity of the charges is never established. While the vast majority of child molestation charges made *outside a divorce context* — normally against a neighbor, relative, or stranger — are ultimately found to be true, charges made *during a custody proceeding* are not nearly so reliable. In less than 50 percent of cases are the allegations sustained.

The charge of child molestation is also subject to frequent abuse because it is such an effective weapon. When the allegation is made, the judge has absolutely no choice but to take action to protect the child from the alleged perpetrator. If the charge is made against dad, no matter how unlikely the charge may seem, the judge must either suspend dad's access to the child or order all access supervised by a third party. If the allegation is made against mom's new mate, the judge must order that mate out of the home or make a custody order so that the child will not be in the home with the accused mate. If it takes months to resolve the matter, the accused party may lose a bond with the child or the child may come to feel abandoned by that person. If the party making a false allegation is on a campaign to alienate the child from the accused parent, the accused parent's long absence from the life of the child is a perfect opportunity to instill in the mind of the child a fear of, and doubt about, the other parent. On the other hand, if the charge turns out to be true, everyone realizes how important it was for the judge to have acted quickly to protect the child's safety.

How to Respond to a Charge of Child Molestation

The only advice that can be given to someone who has indeed molested a child is to retain a capable criminal attorney and seek help from a therapist. If you have molested your own child and want to reunite with the child, it is a long and painful process. You can obtain help from organizations such as Parents United. Child molestation that occurs within the family is frequently brought on by stress, alcohol or other substances, or temporary emotional factors. In these cases, the perpetrator is not a pedophile or a predator from whom children must always be shielded. However, the perpetrator must realize that severe and irreparable emotional harm has been done to the victim and make every effort at rehabilitation to insure that the crime will never occur again.

If you are innocent but falsely charged with molestation, there are steps you can take to help establish your innocence. You will first want to cooperate fully with the authorities. You should insist on a polygraph test even if one is not offered. Although not admissible into evidence in court, a result indicating your innocence will improve your relationship with law enforcement and can at least be mentioned to the judge in an effort to get resolution of the charge on a fast track.

You may also want to ask the judge to appoint an attorney or attorney guardian *ad litem* for the alleged child-victim. This has two advantages. First, the child's attorney can help to prevent the case from taking months or years to resolve. One of the dangers in a case involving a molestation charge against a parent is that once the family court judge has acted to suspend the access of the accused to the children, law enforcement or those charged with investigating the case may put the case on the back burner because the child is no longer "at risk." This is a myopic view, but the authorities often fail to consider the emotional damage to a child that occurs when the child is deprived of access to an innocent parent. They think of a child's best interests only in terms of protecting the child from an immediate threat from the alleged perpetrator. An attorney for the child can go to those investigating the case and insist that the investigation proceed apace; if it does not, she may join with the accused in asking the family court judge to hold a hearing and make a finding on the truth of the charge regardless of whether or not the authorities have completed their investigation. The attorney can make it clear that it is not acceptable for the investigation to proceed with glacial speed because it is not in the best interests of the child-client. Second, an attorney with insight and access to the child may conclude that the molestation did not occur and seek to persuade the judge that you are innocent of the charges. Normally the judge will appoint any willing attorney the parents agree on.

It may also be wise to ask the judge to order the alleged child-victim into counseling. However, here you need to be *very careful*. Some so-called victim or victim-witness counselors will presume the truth of the charge before it has been established and the child will be asked each week to confront sexual and prurient subjects.

I recently presided over a case where the children's therapist, assuming the truth of charges that were very much in doubt, on each visit led the children into a rendition of all that they had suffered at the hands of their father. After many weeks of discussing sexual matters, the children seemed inordinately preoccupied with sexual matters. The children's therapist, who had absolutely no information about the father, viewed the preoccupation as the result of the molestation. A far more skilled and qualified clinician suggested that it might be time for the children to have a "rest" from their weekly guided tour of prurient topics, as a way to lessen their preoccupation with sexual subjects and activities. The respite was ordered, and the children began to focus on how much they missed their father. It is not unusual for children to believe that they were molested when indeed they were not. These are often very young children who do not really understand the implications of what they have been taught to say, or older children who have been convinced by one parent that essentially innocent and affectionate conduct was actually prurient in its motivation.

However, if you can obtain from the judge the appointment of an experienced therapist who has an open mind on the allegations, that therapist may conclude that there is absolutely nothing in what the children say that would support the charges. Or he may recognize that the children have literally been programmed by the other parent to repeat the charges without actually believing them or really understanding them.

The custody evaluator in family court will not likely arrive at a conclusion on the truth of the molestation charge without talking with the children's therapist, and it will be necessary to obtain a waiver of the child's therapist-patient privilege of confidentiality before the therapist can talk to anyone.

It is not terribly difficult to discern whether children who allege that they have been molested actually understand and believe the charges that they are making. A child who does not understand or believe that the molestation which he or she is describing actually occurred will often describe the events with what psychologists call "flat affect" — showing no emotion while describing the events. The child who has been programmed by the accusing parent will also repeat the events in a rote or memorized way.

Finally, children who do not understand the nature of the allegations they are making or their seriousness may begin to accuse many others of having molested them. In a molestation case over which I presided, the child, who at first had accused the father of molesting her, soon came to charge all aunts, uncles, grandparents, brothers, sisters, and some strangers of having engaged in the same acts. Either that child had absorbed a totally false belief system about the father's family from the mother who made the charges, or the father's family was indeed a family grouping of persons more dangerous to children than had ever previously been documented. It should be noted that the children's therapist, who had accepted the truth of the allegations without sufficient evidence to justify such a belief, clung tenaciously to the view that the father was guilty of the molestation and the charges against all of the other family members were just normal exaggeration to be expected from children.

A motion for psychological evaluations of both parents is crucial to the falsely accused parent. False charges of child molestation may often be the result of serious personality disorders on the part of the parent bringing the charges. A psychological evaluation may reveal that the accusing parent has no ability to see her own needs apart from the children's, or has a serious personality disorder, while the accused parent may test out as essentially having no emotional instability. Such information will be very helpful to the judge in determining the truth of the charges.

If false charges were brought against you and you were not the primary custodial parent, you may wish to bring a motion for an award of primary custody at the conclusion of the investigation. If the judge concludes that the charges were false, he may also conclude that they were the product of a psychological profile to which children should not be subjected and which may not be amenable to treatment.

Finally, if you are in a jurisdiction in which the statutes provide that the parent bringing a false charge of child abuse may be ordered to pay the attorney fees incurred by the accused parent in refuting the charge, you should make a motion for such an award of sanctions at the same time that you move for a change of custody.

DO'S AND DON'TS

Do . . .

• Immediately report to the authorities any allegation of abuse made to you by your child.

• Find an experienced child therapist to help the child work through the child's feelings and fears as a result of the abuse.

• If you are falsely accused of molesting a child, cooperate fully with law enforcement's investigation of the charges, and, if a polygraph test is not offered to you, insist that you be permitted to take one.

• If you are falsely accused of molesting a child, seek the appointment of an attorney or attorney guardian ad litem for the child, a therapist for the child, and a Ph.D. psychologist to do psychological evaluations of both you and the accusing parent.

Don't . . .

• Don't agree to the appointment of a therapist for the alleged child-victim unless you are convinced that the therapist will keep an open mind on the charges until all the evidence is in.

• Don't forget that a *capable* child therapist can tell if a child making an allegation of having been molested actually believes and understands the charges.

• If the court finds that you are falsely accused of molesting your child, don't fail to consider making a motion for primary custody of the child, which will be heard when the investigation is complete.

• Don't overlook a motion for attorney fees incurred in defending against the charge against you if the statutes of your jurisdiction permit such an award to an innocent parent who is falsely accused.

9.

Domestic Violence:
Things Have Changed

Many of my colleagues believe that there is more domestic violence in our society than in years past. I'm not sure that they are correct. It may only be that more physical spousal abuse is being *reported*. Women are finally saying "We're not going to take it any more."

Moreover, abused women have more protection available to them than ever before. They need not fear that reporting the crime will just lead to more abuse that they are helpless to stop. There are more shelters in which battered women can seek refuge from an abusive spouse. These shelters also offer excellent legal advice on how to access the court system to protect oneself. There are also many more counselors available to victims of abuse who will help them escape the financial and emotional dependency that led them to remain with the abuser for longer than they should have.

There has been a major change in the attitude of police, as they have come under pressure by women's groups and society generally to take domestic violence more seriously. The officer who, fifteen years ago, would have told the abused spouse to discuss the matter with her pastor now places the abuser under arrest, puts him in handcuffs, and hauls him off to jail. If the abuser has a history of such conduct, a judge may set a substantial bail that the abuser cannot make, at least not until the victim has a chance to set up some defenses.

There is no doubt that judges, too, are much more sensitive to issues of abuse and the needs of abused women. The so-called "diversion" programs that were the rage in the 1980s have been replaced by substantial jail sentences. The diversion programs were a sham: The batterer would go to some classes on anger management or domestic violence, and when these were completed, the charges were dismissed. These programs sent the message that abuse of one's spouse was no more serious than a traffic infraction or possession of less than an ounce of marijuana.

It is important that men admit that the vast majority — probably over 90 percent — of abusers are men. We must recognize as well that over 50 percent of abuse involves the abuse of alcohol or drugs. In the same way that women must face the reality that most child alienation is by women, men must face their responsibility for domestic violence. If we don't admit the truth about problems, they are more difficult to solve.

How to Protect Yourself and Your Children

If you are a victim of domestic violence, call the police. If you are not willing to take this basic step of self-protection, you will not be able to free yourself from what is for most families — and has likely become for you — a cycle of violence, sorrow, forgiveness, and then more violence. When the police arrive, *do not deny that you have been abused* because you believe that the abuser is "sorry" and you want to save the marriage or relationship. There is no evidence that one call to the police instills in an abuser such fear that he will cease the abuse and seek help. Indeed, when you falsely recant when the police arrive, all evidence available suggests that you have actually *reduced* the chances of saving the relationship. The abuse will soon be repeated over and over until you finally *do* have the courage to put an end to it. The abuser will not have faced either the seriousness of the crime, your determination to protect yourself, or his need to deal with a major flaw in his character. Moreover, such false alarms make your next call for help less credible to the police. When the police arrive, *insist upon an arrest.*

One of the primary reasons a woman may recant when the officer arrives (or at time of trial) is the fear that she and the children will be out on the street and she will be unable to support the family. Another is that the husband threatens to take the children away if she leaves. Even highly educated wives need information about how the shelter system works, what the law really is, and where she can go for advice, protection, and shelter.

After the abuser has been arrested, you should immediately seek a court order restraining the abuser from coming near you or even contacting you on the telephone. At the same time you need an order awarding you temporary custody of the children, and if they have also been subjected to abuse, an order that the abuser stay away from the children. If the abuser is likely to be released from jail soon, or for some reason will be cited but not arrested, obtain an order than he immediately vacate the family residence, taking only his clothing and personal effects with him. These remedies are available whether or not you are married to the abuser.

An attorney can obtain these orders for you in a matter of hours, but *in most jurisdictions you do not need an attorney.* Advisors at *women's shelters* or connected with *domestic violence hot lines* or *counseling centers* can either show you how to fill out the necessary papers or can tell you where the help is available. In some states the officer who makes the arrest can telephone a judge, who will authorize the officer to give you a temporary emergency restraining order and register it with other law enforcement agencies. In progressive states, *family courts* have help centers where volunteers or court employees will help you fill out an application for a restraining order as well as a motion for support for you and the children.

Unless the abuser pleads guilty, you will be called upon to testify in court. The victim's testimony is almost always needed for a conviction because there are usually no witnesses to domestic violence other than the abuser, the victim, and sometimes the children. The abuser will almost always seek to persuade the victim not to testify. The effort is often made with promises that the abuser is a "changed man" and wants to reestablish the relationship. Or there may be threats of greater violence against the victim if she testifies.

Is dismissal of the charges against the abuser a danger to the victim? Yes, because many abusers will not or cannot change their reliance on force to express frustration or to get their way unless they learn to deal with the problem in behavior modification classes that will be made a condition of probation after a conviction. Few abusers ever attend such classes voluntarily, but will do so to avoid a return to jail or when such classes are made a condition of access to their children.

Should You Reveal Abuse to the Custody Evaluator?

As stated in chapter 2, in the past many victims of domestic violence simply did not raise the subject during custody evaluations. Some experts say that victims feared being looked upon as "that kind of woman." There seems to have been the feeling that victims of spousal abuse were viewed by others as dependent, incapable, or perhaps "trashy." In addition, domestic violence was a subject that the evaluator would just as soon avoid. The subject was thought to provoke great emotion and bitterness, but was not seen as terribly relevant to the issue of child custody.

Today, a careful custody evaluator will ask the mother if she has been the victim of abuse, and considers the issue quite relevant to custody. You owe it to your children to answer truthfully if you have been abused, and to raise the subject if the custody evaluator does not inquire. Someone capable of using violence on his spouse or mate may be capable of using violence against his children. Moreover, you need to give the custody evaluator a complete picture. If you fled the family home out of fear for your safety, it may appear that you willfully abandoned your children. Indeed, in a separate meeting with the evaluator, your mate may be alleging that both he and the children were abandoned for selfish reasons. (It is common for an evaluator to meet with the parents both together and separately.)

When physical abuse is alleged, the custody evaluator will consider a number of options that would not be explored if the information were concealed. The evaluator may wish to meet with the parents separately rather than together. (Indeed, some jurisdictions require separate mediation and evaluation when abuse is alleged. The victim is not demeaned by having to meet in the same room with the abuser.) The evaluator may order the children into counseling, especially if they have witnessed the abuse. The abuser may be ordered into anger management classes or domestic violence rehabilitation treatment as a condition of access to the children. If the abuser is given access to the children, the exchange may be structured so that the victim is not in danger; for example, in a public place, or by pickup and drop off at school or day care, so that the parents do not meet face to face.

When abuse is involved, it is important to bring to the evaluation as much documentary evidence of the abuse as possible. Abusers often have a calmer and more confident demeanor than the victim who fears for her physical safety, and that demeanor can be mistaken for truthfulness. The best documentation, of course, will be conviction records for abuse or battery against the victim or any other person. Next best are police reports of arrests, investigations, and/or incidents. Even records that a report was made but no action was taken by the police can be helpful. Affidavits under oath by those who have witnessed the abuse or the physical marks of abuse can be persuasive (e.g., medical records), especially if the person is available by telephone to talk to the custody evaluator.

Warn the Courthouse Deputies in Advance That a Dangerous Person Will Be Present at the Courthouse

If you are afraid for your safety or your very life, or that of your children, and especially if you believe that the abuser is in possession of a weapon, you may wish to take police reports or conviction records, a few days prior to the hearing, to the bailiff of the judge who will hear your case. The bailiff and those officers responsible for security at the courthouse entrance sincerely appreciate knowing if a dangerous person will be in the courtroom. They will be even more appreciative in those jurisdictions that refuse to protect the attorneys, the public, and court employees by installing metal detectors.

Approximately ten years ago, before my court installed a metal detector, a litigant went through an entire mediation in the courthouse with a large .45 caliber handgun concealed in a lunch pail. It was discovered when a deputy asked him to open the lunch pail before he entered the courtroom. With advance warning that a dangerous person will be in the courtroom, my bailiff often arranged for an extra deputy to be present during the period of danger, and notified the deputies at the metal detector. Our Family Court Services unit regularly sends notices to all deputies in the courthouse when their records indicate that a person with a history of violence will be in the courthouse for a mediation or an evaluation.

What About Your Safety After a Court Hearing?

After a hearing, mediation, or evaluation has been completed, you should feel free to ask the bailiff or other deputy to escort you to your automobile if you feel that you are not safe leaving the courthouse alone. This is a courtesy that many bailiffs extend to abuse victims daily. The bailiff will order the abuser to immediately leave the courthouse, and then when court is in recess or the calendar is complete, the bailiff will escort the abused parent or mate to her car. Even the occasional "lazy" deputy sheriff will not want to risk the liability that may be incurred if your request is denied and you are harmed on the way to your automobile. If for any reason this courtesy is not provided by law enforcement in your jurisdiction, you may wish to contact women's groups and anti-domestic violence organizations. They may well provide you with a volunteer to go to court with you to help assure your safety. (The mere presence of a companion is a strong deterrent to violence.) The group may also want to raise publicly — in local newspapers and in meetings with community leaders and law enforcement — the issue of why this courtesy is not provided.

If there is one bit of important advice I have for someone who is in a quandary over whether or not to reveal that she is a victim of domestic violence, it is the following: *To be the victim of abuse cannot possibly be a character flaw. To conceal abuse, so that you subject yourself and your children to further violence, may well be.* Remember, judges and mental health professionals are light-years past such attitudes as "She asked for it," or "She knows how to push his buttons." Today, *nothing* is considered a justification for physical abuse.

How the Law Treats the Custody Rights of Abusers

Many states have enacted laws that limit the rights of access of spouse abusers to a child. While no state has said that one guilty of spouse abuse is forever disqualified from having access to the child, some states have statutes that require a judge to make specific findings before custody can be awarded to someone who has abused the other parent. Or a state may require that the abuser present evidence to overcome a presumption that custody not be awarded to that person. Or the abuser may be required to meet a higher burden of proof on the custody issue than the victim parent must meet.

For example, in California, the Family Code declares that domestic violence is detrimental to a child, and that the safety of a child and all family members takes priority over the state's policy of assuring that children have frequent and continuing contact with both parents. Moreover, a history of abuse must be considered by a judge in determining a child's best interests. If a judge makes an award of custody or visitation to an abuser, the court must also find that there was no reasonable alternative and explain why such an award is in the child's best interests. Finally, in a case with a history of spousal abuse, the court must consider requiring supervised visitation, suspending visitation, or even denying visitation altogether.

As a practical matter, those guilty of abuse of a type that can cause serious injury to the victim are seldom granted primary custody of children. They don't make very good parents.

DO'S AND DON'TS

Do . . .

• The moment abuse starts, call the police as soon as you can get away.

• After the abuser is arrested, immediately seek a restraining order from the court that orders him to stay away and not make telephone contact. Serve the restraining order on him before he is released from jail.

• Support the prosecutor in obtaining a conviction by voluntarily testifying at the trial.

• Tell the custody evaluator if you have been the victim of physical abuse.

• If available, bring to the evaluation documentary proof that you have been abused.

• If the abuser is a continuing danger to you, give advance warning to the bailiff responsible for safety in the courtroom in which you will appear that the abuser will be in the courthouse for a hearing or mediation on a given day. Simply dropping off copies of police reports with the date of the hearing attached is sufficient notice.

• If the deputies at the courthouse in your jurisdiction do not provide abuse victims with an escort to their automobile when they leave the courthouse, contact a women's shelter or anti-domestic violence organization and seek a volunteer to accompany you to the courthouse.

Don't . . .

• Don't overlook women's shelters as an excellent source of legal advice and help as well as supportive counseling, even though you do not need to reside there.

• When the police arrive, don't recant the allegations of domestic violence you made in your 911 call.

• If you are in fear for your safety if you leave the courthouse alone, don't fail to ask the bailiff or other deputy to escort you to your car.

• Don't believe that it is a character flaw to be the victim of domestic violence. No one believes that anymore. The flaw is in the failure to take the actions necessary to end it forever.

• Don't fail to obtain an award of child custody when you obtain an initial restraining order from the police or the court.

10.

Parental Alienation

arental alienation is an effort by one parent to cause a child to fear or dislike the other parent. For example, when the father attempts to obtain greater time with the child, the mother may tell the child, "Your father doesn't really love you or want to see you. He only wants to spend more time with you so the judge will lower his child support." Or, "We can't take the trip to Disneyland this month. Your father is late again with your child support." Similarly, a critical father may tell the children, "Your mother has run off with her boyfriend. She cares more about him than she does about us. Pretty soon she will want him to be your father."

Parental alienation occurs in varying degrees of intensity. Some occasional disparagement of the other parent in the presence of the children probably occurs in the vast majority of divorces or paternity disputes. At the other end of the spectrum, judges see parents who attempt to fill the child's head with hatred of the other parent on an almost daily basis. It may occur during custody litigation as an effort to obtain a primary custody award or an ally in the litigation. It may occur shortly after a permanent custody award is made or a long time thereafter, as a result of spite or vindictiveness or in an effort to change the prior custody award.

Some efforts to alienate a child from the other parent are so gross and obvious as to be apparent even to those uninitiated in the subject, as in the examples above. Other attempts at child alienation are more subtle, and perhaps even more effective. Asking a child to keep secrets from the other parent is a favorite ploy. "Don't tell your dad, but you are going to have a brother next March." Or, "I would like to take you skiing, but this is your mom's weekend." Or, in reference to dad's new mate, "That woman can't tell you what to do. She is not your mother and has no rights over you." Or, very subtly, "Your mom won't have time for you next weekend, but you and I will go to the beach."

Parental alienation takes many forms, of course, but before we continue this discussion, let me clarify my framework. For purposes of this chapter, it is assumed that both parents are essentially responsible adults, fully capable of caring for their child(ren) in a manner you and I (and the family court of jurisdiction) would agree is in the best interests of the child(ren). Thus any attempt by one parent to alienate the child from the other would be out of line and reprehensible. There are, of course, those parents whose lifestyles and/or behavior patterns are so disreputable that the other parent's efforts at protecting could actually be considered in the best interests of the child(ren). Those are not the people we're talking about here.

Evidence of Parental Alienation

"Parental alienation syndrome" is a phrase used by mental health professionals to represent the characteristics exhibited by a child who has been turned against one parent by the other. These include fear of the victim parent, refusal to visit that parent, dislike of the parent's new mate, refusal to obey the victim parent or that parent's new mate, and a hypercritical attitude toward the other parent (who can't do anything to please the child).

A good clue that parental alienation is at work is that the child's language is inappropriate for the age of the child. For example, a 5-year-old says, "My dad isn't sensitive to children's needs," or "My dad is self-centered." Another indication of alienation is that the child is suddenly interested in topics that never concern a child of that age. For example, "My mom is a poor housekeeper and doesn't feed me healthy food." Where do you think he got that idea? Or, "My dad wants to spend more time with me so he won't have to pay so much child support." Or, "My dad spends all his money on his new girlfriend."

As you can see, parental alienation may be fairly easy to uncover if the opportunity arises. Indeed, when the child is asked how he knows such a thing, the child invariably says, "My mom/dad told me." Such remarks by a child as, "My dad screams at me a lot," or "My dad hits me too much," are consistent with a child's concerns and are appropriately stated. While the child may be repeating what mom has said, the custody evaluator certainly cannot conclude that from the remark itself.

Sometimes a statement made by the parent in the courtroom will suggest to the judge to be alert for possible alienation. For example (referring to a 5-year-old), "My daughter doesn't want to visit and I can't make her." At this point the judge knows that she must determine whether the child is being alienated from the father or some conduct by the father is threatening to the child. If one parent keeps demanding that the judge talk to the child, that's at least an indication that the requesting parent believes the child will side with that parent's view of what a parenting plan should be. But of course the next question is *why* is the child siding with one parent? There are a number of possible answers; parental alienation is only one.

What Can Be Done About Parental Alienation?

At this point, let me reiterate a view expressed earlier in this book. I believe that efforts at alienation will be unsuccessful if the parent who is the potential victim remains above the fray and refuses to become involved in the criticism game. As long as the potential victim acts as a loving parent and refuses to criticize the other parent or discuss the criticism at length, the child will not be successfully turned against the victim parent. Children are smart and have an innate sense of fairness. If the conduct of the potential victim parent does not fit the description given to the child by the alienating parent, the child will continue to feel secure with the potential victim parent and the effort at alienation will fail.

Most mental health professionals, custody evaluators, and judges believe that parental alienation of a child from the other parent may be considered a form of child abuse. An alienated child may grow up with a skewed view of adults, of the gender of the parent from whom the child is alienated, and of the proper role of a parent in a child's life. The child's ability to trust is likely impaired. Serious emotional injury may occur, making it more difficult for the child to later establish a lasting relationship with a mate. On a more material level, an alienated parent is far less likely to pay child support willingly for the young child who holds the parent in disdain, and is not likely to voluntarily pay for a college education after the child reaches majority (and the court loses jurisdiction to order support).

Sometimes nothing can be done to correct the situation. This is true of the alienated teenager. Teenagers are past the age at which the court can dictate a parenting plan or at which counseling is apt to help the child develop a more objective view of both parents. Indeed, many teenagers will refuse even to meet in a counselor's office with the parent from whom the teenager has been alienated. Experienced judges and custody evaluators take some solace in the fact that alienated children, after they grow into adulthood and attain greater objectivity, often reconcile or reunify with their disdained parents.

The judge or the custody evaluator should warn parents early in the court process of the damage that alienation will do to a child. Some courts have an orientation program or other mandatory parental education sessions for those in custody disputes. During these sessions the parents will be advised of a number of acts that may emotionally harm their children. Alienation is but one.

As a last resort, a judge can award custody to the parent who is the victim of the alienation, and require the other parent's visitation to be supervised by a professional supervisor, who will monitor what is said to the child. In some cases, access of the alienating parent may be suspended for a period to give the child a chance to recover from the "brainwashing" campaign to which the child may have been subjected for a substantial period. In some states, statutes require that the ability of the parents to share a child — *and support the other parent's relationship with the child* — be one of the factors that the judge must consider in determining which parent, if either, should be granted an award of primary custody.

With younger children, judges are still constrained in certain instances from removing custody from an alienating parent. If the child does not have a strong bond with the victim parent, for example, an immediate change in custody will be terribly traumatic for the child. A gradual increase in the victim parent's time with the child, while desirable, may not be possible if the alienating parent refuses to follow court orders.

Of course, the alienating parent who loses primary custody of the child is generally quite angry with the judge and the court system that has produced the result. The alienator almost always believes her own view of the other parent and feels that the child must be told "the truth." She will not accept the fact that objective observers do not see the other parent as a threat to the emotional or physical safety of the child.

If the parent who is attempting to alienate the child is not the parent with primary custody, remedies are much easier to come by. The alienating parent can be placed on supervised visitation, or in an extreme case, visitation can be suspended. The short-term trauma to the child of either remedy is unlikely to outweigh the long-term benefit of putting an end to the alienation campaign.

Alienation During Abduction

Child abductors are an excellent — if extreme — example of how difficult it is for the court to remove custody from a parent engaged in the worst form of alienation. If the abduction is successful for a year or so, the child's memories of the victim parent may be vague, and the child is likely to be terrified of that parent. The abductor has had a substantial period of time to instill in the child a great distrust of the other parent and all that parent represents. Even when the child has a good bond with the victim parent, a change in custody will often result in some short-term trauma for the child. The child has no way of knowing that the things said about the victim parent are not true and that the parent is not the villain who has been described to the child. In almost all cases where the judge is considering taking primary custody away from an alienating parent, the judge must balance some short-term discomfort for the child against the long-term consequences of alienation. The custody evaluator will be doing the same thing; the evaluator knows that this consideration will be uppermost in the mind of the judge. The need to free a child from a totally false belief system that might handicap the child throughout life is more important than short discomfort the child may feel; the child's long-term well-being is the overriding consideration.

In these situations, it is not unusual for an alienator to drag a child from therapist to therapist, in an effort to find an ally who will assist in convincing the child and the judge that the other parent is a threat to the child. The welfare of the child makes it almost imperative that such a process be brought to an end.

Proving That the Other Parent Is Alienating the Child

There are certain steps that an innocent parent can take to help prove that the other parent is attempting to alienate the child. As noted earlier, the first step is not to be drawn into the alienation contest. If you do take the bait, it will make the efforts of the other parent more successful, and you will lose your standing before the court as the victim in the matter. (Of course, the *real* victim is the child.)

You should ask the judge to order the child into therapy with an experienced *child therapist*. It may be a good idea to suggest that the judge choose the therapist because you want a person who will have great credibility with the judge. Over a series of sessions, the child is almost certain to say things to the therapist that will indicate that one parent's conduct is inappropriate and harmful to the child. The therapist is apt to report this to the custody evaluator, who will then be alerted to the problem. If the therapist's concerns are communicated in this way, you have not embroiled the therapist in the litigation any more than necessary to alert the custody evaluator to the problem. The custody evaluator may then undertake to investigate the situation and may recommend to the judge a change in primary custody or supervised access, or both.

It may also be helpful to ask the judge to appoint an *attorney* to represent the child. Custody evaluators, especially those in the public sector, seldom have time to act as caseworkers and/or to see the child at regular intervals. On the other hand, the child's attorney may do just that, and may obtain a better picture of the pressures being brought on your child than the evaluator will have. One of the first duties of attorneys for children is to inform the judge or the evaluator of any dangers to a child-client. Thus if the attorney comes to believe that alienation is taking place, you can be certain that someone with the authority to act will be notified.

Finally, you may find it helpful if a *special master* is appointed in the case. A special master in custody cases is often a mental health professional appointed by the court and given the authority to rule on disputes between the parents over child-related issues. The special master's job is to resolve disputes by the parents over vacations, health care, education, transportation, visitation, and other aspects of parenting without the need for the parents to spend the money to return to court each time a dispute arises. Of course any ruling by the special master, if objected to by one parent, must be approved by the court. But an experienced special master who sees the parties and the child a number of times may, like the attorney for the child or the therapist, be able to get a better handle on the dynamics of the relationship between child and parents than the judge or your custody evaluator, both of whom have hundreds of cases a year to resolve.

The use of mental health professionals as special masters (called "referees" in some jurisdictions) in custody cases has become very popular in parts of California and is beginning to slowly penetrate other jurisdictions as well. The judge, however, may not have the authority to appoint a special master without the consent of both parents. But don't assume that you can't get the consent of the offending parent. Parents who seek to alienate children from the other parent are often acting as they do because they believe in the truth of everything they tell the child, and they do not see the long-term harmful effects on the child.. They see the other parent as being to blame for all discord and any emotional problems the child may have. They believe the special master as a potential ally who will see things their way and make rulings accordingly. Parents engaged in the most egregious conduct, from the perspective of an objective observer, often see the special master as an opportunity to achieve quick justice and vindication at an affordable price. They often will agree to the appointment of a special master without hesitation.

Unfortunately, there are significant costs for the assistance of therapists, attorneys, and special masters in the proof that conduct by the other parent is harmful to your child. The more modest the financial resources of a victim parent, the less help will be available and the longer it will take to expose alienation to the judge if, indeed, it is ever exposed.

DO'S AND DON'TS

Do . . .

• If you believe that the other parent is attempting to alienate your child from you, it may be wise to request that the court appoint an attorney for the child and to seek a court order that your child see a child therapist on a regular basis.

• If you are the parent target of child alienation, and are in a jurisdiction where the court appoints mental health professionals to act as special masters who make findings in custody cases, consider asking the judge to appoint a special master for your case.

Don't . . .

• Don't respond to alienation efforts of the other parent by starting an alienation campaign of your own or by disparaging the other parent to the child. Continue to be available for visits, and document your availability. Take a friend to the pick-up point even if you believe the other parent will not bring the child. Or, request that the exchange take place at a fast-food restaurant. Many fast-food places date and time-stamp their receipts. If you buy a soda when you arrive, you have proof that you were there.

• Don't tell the judge your young child doesn't want to visit with the other parent and you can't make the child go. If your child appears frightened of the other parent apart from anything you may have said or done, simply point out to the judge or evaluator that the child seems frightened of the other parent. Let them investigate the matter.

• Don't expect the court to attempt to change primary custody of a teenager in order to prevent alienation by the custodial parent. It is too late to reverse the process.

• Don't continually demand that the judge talk to the child.

• Don't think that the proof of alienation by the other parent will not be expensive.

11.

Will the Court Be Fair?

Gender Bias, Forum Shopping, and Challenges

Judges are human, not computers or ATM machines, and all humans are the products of their unique heredity, past experiences, and environment. Since these factors determine our belief systems, it is really no surprise that one judge may place greater importance on a mother in a child's day-to-day life, while another judge may emphasize the structure and limits a strong father can provide. Nevertheless, despite the imperfections of human judges, I suspect that most people would not want a custody decision made by a computer. And even that approach doesn't eliminate all possible bias. Whoever programs the computer must make decisions based upon their understanding and experience.

Bias on the Bench?

In past years, fathers have been the most vocal in their claims of gender bias in the courts. Many fathers who have been through the court system in a paternity or divorce case believe that the courts are biased in favor of women, and especially mothers. I think that many men who enter the court system have a working assumption that they are the "nonpreferred gender," the title a father in a recent custody matter in my court gave to himself. On the other hand, women's groups do not see preference for mom as the custodial parent to be a "bias," but a justified cultural assumption.

Some arguments made to support charges of gender bias in the courts simply cannot pass careful scrutiny. For example, some fathers argue that the fact that mothers are awarded custody approximately 75 percent of the time is evidence of gender bias. That is nonsense. Most custody cases are settled by *agreed* custody awards. It is customary for parents who have had a traditional family structure, where mom was the homemaker and dad the breadwinner, to agree that mom will be the primary custodian of the children. It often makes good sense because she has been the primary nurturing parent and the children are likely to rely on her to meet their daily needs. Even if these cases go to a hearing, for the judge to award primary custody to the mother is certainly not evidence of gender bias but a reflection of the nature of the prior family relationships before the parents separated.

However, there is some evidence of bias — in favor of women as primary caregivers — in family courts, according to a 1992 study of 282 child custody cases conducted by psychologists at the University of California at San Diego. One should keep in mind that these findings were collateral to the primary purpose of the study, which was to determine those factors which most influenced judges in their determination of child custody awards. However, the study revealed that the father's chance of receiving a primary custody award was enhanced when his post-separation living arrangements were such that a woman was present in his home. This was true whether that person was a wife, girlfriend, or the father's mother. In addition, when the children expressed a preference for the mother, decisions in favor of the mother were much more frequent. Awards of joint custody were insignificant under those circumstances. When the children expressed a preference for the father, a significant number of awards were for joint custody as opposed to primary custody.

Some of my fellow judges have indicated to me that they must be vigilant not to let gender bias cause them to deny or award spousal support to an able-bodied man who is unemployed for some justifiable reason. Others have confided that it is more difficult to order a woman into jail for the same offense for which a man would be incarcerated. A judge must be very careful not to unconsciously reduce a spousal support award for the husband below the level at which the award would have been made for a wife in the same circumstances. It seems to me that the kind of gender bias that one recognizes and seeks to correct is not nearly so harmful as biases that we do not recognize.

It may well be that both men and women judges have feelings that young children need a mother in their life if at all possible. Prior to 1970, gender bias was written into law in some states through a provision that primary custody of children of tender years was to be awarded to the mother unless she was found to be unfit. This was called the "Tender Years Doctrine." However, an appreciation of what mothers can offer to children is not the type of gross gender bias that most litigants fear. Women fear the judge who does not believe it is proper for women to be employed outside the home and would let that view influence a custody decision. A temporarily unemployed husband does not want to be in front of a judge who believes that spousal support is for women only. One interesting finding in the UC San Diego study is that the longer a father continued to contest custody, the greater was the chance that he would prevail. Although somewhat speculative, perhaps this shows that any bias that may exist in favor of mothers is certainly no more than a presumption that can be overcome by the facts of a specific case.

What does all this mean for the litigant? As suggested elsewhere in this book, the capable custody attorney knows the local judges and how they are apt to respond to certain facts. I continually stress to attorneys in lectures on family law, "Know your local judges." The need to be aware of the leanings of various judges who might hear your case is also another good reason for you to retain an attorney who practices regularly in your jurisdiction.

Should You Shop for a Judge?

Should you make an effort maneuver your case in front of a judge who will provide a friendlier forum for your case than some other judge? That strategy decision should be left primarily in the hands of your attorney.

Judges refer to the effort to move a case to or away from a particular judge as "forum shopping." It is seen by judges as disruptive to a court's effort to maintain even workloads between judges, and violative of the view judges hold that any litigant can receive a fair trial in front of any judge of their particular court.

Thus judges do everything they can to prevent forum shopping. Attorneys, on the other hand, engage in forum shopping to some degree because it is seen to be of benefit to a client. However, you cannot expect your attorney to harm her reputation by making some obvious effort to avoid a judge; that will offend the judge and the courthouse staff. Your attorney is likely to have to work with that judge and staff for many years to come and it is unreasonable to expect her to damage her ability to help other clients by conduct harmful to her reputation in an effort to help a single client.

There are essentially two types of systems by which most courts calendar cases. In the *direct calendaring* system, each case is assigned at random to a single judge and that judge presides over every hearing from the day the case is filed until the case is over (or the judge is assigned to another division of the court). Under a direct calendaring system, your attorney has very little room to maneuver once the assignment is made. However, even under direct calendaring systems, attorneys show a great deal of interest in when a given judge will be on vacation and who will take the place of the vacationing judge.

In the *assignment* system, all cases are called on one "master calendar" by the presiding judge, who then assigns the cases for hearing to other judges who are available that day. Under the latter system of calendaring, your attorney may have some room to maneuver by knowing what judges are available for new assignments on a given day. With that information, your attorney can seek to have your case assigned out for a hearing on that day or continued to another day, depending upon your attorney's view of where she would (or would not) like your case to be heard.

Challenging a Judge — Peremptory

Some states accord to each party the right to one *peremptory challenge* of one judge. In a peremptory challenge, the party alleges — without specifying a reason — that the judge should step down, and the judge must do so. The judge is prohibited from inquiring as to the reasons the challenge is made but must step down if the challenge is timely. There are very strict time limits on how long a party has to exercise the challenge after the judge who will hear the case becomes known. Without going into detail, suffice it to say that you cannot wait until the day of trial to exercise a challenge if the judge is known to you well in advance. In addition, the right to challenge is lost once a judge has ruled on a contested issue of law or fact. You can't wait to see if the judge decides in your favor before exercising a challenge. Most challenges that are rejected by trial judges are rejected because they are not timely filed.

Attorneys are reluctant to use peremptory challenges. There is a feeling among attorneys that the judge will be angered and the attorney must continue to challenge that judge in every case so long as the attorney is in practice and the judge is on the bench. It is commonly believed that the judge will hold the challenge against the attorney in future rulings. I do not agree. The general reaction I see among judges is one of hurt and disappointment. The judge would like to ask the attorney the reason for filing the challenge so that if the judge has done something inappropriate in the eyes of the attorney, the judge will have an opportunity to correct the practice. However, the judge is not permitted to inquire into the reasons a peremptory challenge was filed. Although some judges might hold a grudge, I suspect that they are a small minority.

Of course, you do not want to exercise a peremptory challenge unless you know where your case may be sent. Whatever the characteristic of the judge that causes your attorney to file the challenge, you could wind up in front of a judge with a reputation for even more of the characteristic you wish to avoid. Indeed, the judge with the authority to decide where your case is assigned may deliberately send you to a judge who, from your point of view, is worse than the challenged judge. For many years in my county, if the district attorney challenged a lenient judge, the case was sent to a more lenient judge, and if defense counsel challenged a judge known for tough sentencing, the case went to a tougher judge. If you know that after a challenge you will be sent to the clerk to obtain a random assignment, your attorney must know who is in the pool from which your next judge will be selected. In short, if you challenge Judge Yuk, you don't want to wind up with Judge Double Yuk.

Challenging a Judge — Cause

In every state a judge may be challenged *for cause*. Unlike the peremptory challenge, you must prove what you allege about the judge. There are a whole series of reasons for which a judge may be challenged for cause, having to do with the judge's relationship with a party or one of the attorneys or a conflict of interest. These challenges seldom need to be formally made, and when they are, the judge will normally willingly step down if the allegations appear correct. The vast majority of challenges for cause, however, are based on an allegation that the judge is either biased, or appears to be biased. Judges strongly resist these challenges. They may be based on something the judge said in an offhand remark. Or the judge may have written something that would lead one to believe that he has made up his mind before the evidence is all in, or perhaps before any evidence has been presented.

The reason most challenges for cause fail is that they are made by disgruntled litigants based upon the rulings of the judge. They contend that the rulings are so misguided that they are evidence that the judge is biased against them. Such a challenge will be unsuccessful because the remedy for an erroneous ruling is the Court of Appeal, not a challenge for bias. This type of challenge based on rulings is another example of attempting to challenge the judge after you find that the rulings are adverse to you. It is not unreasonable for the courts to deny such challenges as a form of forum shopping.

Challenges for cause must be heard by a judge other than the one challenged. Normally the ruling will be based on affidavits by the party claiming bias and an affidavit by the judge in response. There are also time limits in most states for challenges for cause. After the facts giving rise to the challenge are discovered, the challenge must be made promptly. If you wait until the day of trial, in many states the trial will proceed forward and your challenge will be heard after the trial, or the judge may be authorized by statute to strike the challenge if it is untimely. If the order striking the challenge as untimely is proper, the challenge will never be heard by another judge.

Almost any challenge for gender bias is likely to be unsuccessful. Unless the judge has made some ill-advised and intemperate remark, these challenges are often based upon rulings which are alleged to show gender bias. However, if rulings are based on gender bias, again, the proper remedy is the Court of Appeal.

DO'S AND DON'TS

Do . . .

• Understand that some judges have strong feelings that young children need a mother in their lives. This is not the kind of gender bias that most litigants fear.

• Retain an attorney familiar with the tendencies and leanings of the judges of the court who will hear your case.

• Keep careful track of how long you have to file a peremptory challenge after you know the name of the judge who will hear your case.

• Let your attorney decide if a peremptory challenge should be used.

Don't . . .

• Don't believe that gender bias in the courts is the reason statistics show more custody awards are made to mothers than to fathers.

• Don't expect your attorney to injure his or her reputation by using an obvious and inappropriate tactic to avoid a given judge.

• Don't base a challenge for cause on the judge's rulings.

• Don't use a peremptory challenge without some idea of where your case may end up, unless you believe that the judge you are challenging is the least desirable on the entire court to hear your case.

• Don't expect a challenge for gender bias to be successful.

12.

Child Support

After wavering for several weeks, I finally decided to include a chapter on child support in this book. Essentially a financial issue, child support is often thought of as unrelated to child custody. However, the two issues are linked in a number of ways. Child custody is about the needs of children, and adequate child support is one of their greatest needs. A child raised without adequate support is at a significant disadvantage in life. Inadequate support may mean virtual poverty, and the likelihood of poor schools, poor health care, and a social environment in which the values of education and achievement will take a back seat to the tasks of obtaining food, shelter, and safety. An economically disadvantaged child will be far less likely to attend college, and the chances that he will drop out of school or engage in criminal conduct as a teenager or young adult are dramatically increased.

Absence of solid child support may make the difference, significantly limiting the child's options in life (the occasional "poor kid makes good" story notwithstanding). Only a very small percentage of children raised in poverty are able to find their way to a better life. Even if lack of child support may not mean actual poverty for your child, it will be a very important factor in defining his lifestyle and opportunities.

Child support is also connected to child custody by way of the bond between a child and a parent obligated by law to pay child support. The closer the bond, the more likely that the support will be fully and timely paid. It never ceases to amaze me that custodial parents who thwart the other parent's access to the child fail to see that what they are doing contributes to the other parent's failure to make timely payments of the full amount of support.

Custodial parents who withhold visitation should note the following statistics: Of fathers who have *joint or shared custody*, 90 percent pay child support. Of fathers who have only rights of *visitation*, 79 percent pay child support. But of fathers who have *no visitation or custodial time*, only 45 percent pay child support.

Variations Among the States

My major reservation in attempting to do this chapter about child support is that child support laws differ widely from state to state. I was concerned that finding the law of each state on child support would take 200 hours of research time, which a sitting judge simply cannot afford to give, and the cost of hiring an attorney to research the laws would be astronomical. However, a senior attorney at the California Administrative Office of Courts told me of a book entitled *Child Support Guidelines: Interpretation and Application* by Laura W. Morgan of the National Law Research Group. This group, based in Charlottesville, Virginia, is composed of senior attorneys who are experts in the family law of all 50 states. They do research in family law, normally for attorneys on specific issues. Not only did I use material from Attorney Morgan's book, but when I spoke to her personally, she knew the answer to several other questions off the top of her head. For those questions she could not answer, she produced the answer in less than two weeks. Her book and her efforts on behalf of this book have allowed me to confidently write chapters on child support and attorney fees. I am much indebted to her.

Factors Determining Child Support

In many states, the parenting plan will influence child support. All states now have child support schedules (often called "guidelines," as if they were not really mandatory) that judges are required to use. Various states allow more or less leeway to the judge to deviate from the guideline figure of support. Guidelines are the result of threats by the federal government to lower its contributions to state welfare funds unless a state sets up child support guidelines which will yield the "correct" amount of support. These schedules, at a minimum, are based upon the incomes of one or both parties and the number of children to be supported.

All states have some way of lowering child support as the supporting parent spends more time with the child. A substantial number use a sliding scale that reduces support as a supporting parent's time with the child increases. In the majority of states, however, shared parenting is a factor that allows the judge to deviate from the guideline amount and reduce the level of support. Thus in all states we have the unhappy situation where disputes over visitation are driven as much by financial considerations as by a desire to parent and enjoy a child. This should come as no surprise because in all states supporting parents believe that support is higher — at every level of income — than most obligated parents believe they can reasonably afford to pay. For parents with lower than average income, at least, they are probably right.

At this writing, California alone has based child support on a mathematical formula that must be applied statewide by all judges. As a result, all California family law judges have computers in the courtroom, with programs that apply the formula to the evidence on income, time-sharing, and number of children. In arriving at a child support figure, these programs even take into account the tax shelters a parent may have (that will free up more money for support), as well as the needs of children of another relationship that the paying parent may be obligated to support.

Parent Income and Child Support

Child support set by guideline is especially hard on low-income payers. If a father earning $6,000 net per month is ordered to pay 25 percent of his income for the support of his children, he still has $4,500 remaining to live on. The $1,500 for child support comes out of funds for discretionary spending. When a father who earns $1,000 net per month is ordered to pay 25 percent for child support, the $250 per month is coming out of funds that would ordinarily be earmarked for the necessities of life: food, shelter, and clothing.

States differ widely in the ways that they will permit the judge to award less than guideline support when the supporting party has very low income. In eighteen states, if the supporting parent has income below a set poverty threshold, the award that is presumed correct is a monthly minimum of $50 per child. In other states, a figure of $20 to $50 is a minimum award from which the supporting party cannot seek a downward modification. Under a third approach, in low-income cases the guidelines are discarded and the judge uses her discretion. Most states recognize the concept of a "self-support reserve" in low-income cases. That is, an amount is subtracted from the supporting party's income for that party's own support before child support is calculated.

States vary in how long child support is payable. In some it ends at age 18, in others at 21. In states where the cutoff is at age 18, if a child is still a full-time high school student, support may be extended until the child graduates or turns 19. In states in which support is paid until age 21, a child will be helped to obtain a college education.

New-Mate Income

In most states, new-mate income is not considered in arriving at guideline child support. To say that it is not "considered" is to say that it is not added to a parent's income or used in place of income for a parent who has no income. While several states allow consideration of new-mate income in well-defined and unusual circumstances, others simply say it can never be added to the income of either parent in determining the proper level of child support.

Strong public support has been expressed for laws that prohibit judges from considering the income of a parent's new spouse or mate when setting child support. A new spouse or mate is often very hostile to seeing his or her income go for the support of someone else's children. In states where legislation has been introduced to eliminate new-mate income from consideration in fixing child and spousal support, there has been a ground-swell of public support in favor of the legislation. Legislators were surprised that the issue does not divide people along gender lines. Women, it turns out, resent having their income going for someone else's children just as much as men do. Indeed, it is often the obligated parent's new spouse who is pushing the obligated parent to move for reduced child support.

While no portion of new-mate income may be added to the parent's *income* in arriving at guideline child support, in California at least, case law mandates that where a parent files a joint tax return with a new spouse, the judge is required to use new-mate income in determining the *tax bracket* of that parent. If the *supporting* party is pushed into a higher tax bracket by new-mate income, child support will decrease, because there is less money for child support after taxes are paid. If the *supported* party is pushed into a higher tax bracket by new-mate income, child support will increase, because the supported party has less money to contribute to support the child after taxes are paid. (This increase in support as the supported party's funds decrease applies only to those states where the supported party's income is included in the child support formula.)

High-Income Parents

All states also allow a judge to depart from the schedules when the earnings of the obligated parent are so high that the amount of child support mandated by the schedule would be in excess of what any child needs for support. In a minority of states, the judge sets child support in high-earner cases by determining the needs of the child. However, these needs are those of *a child with the obligated parent's standard of living,* and may include private school tuition, expensive summer camps, music and language lessons, nannies, automobiles, a college fund, and the need to live in a good neighborhood with good schools.

In some of these states the statutes fix a given level of income above which a person is considered a high earner. In other states (including California), the definition of a high earner is for the judge to determine at his or her discretion. The level the judge chooses will depend upon the standard of living in the community, and the expectations the community has for the expense of raising children. In the Silicon Valley of California, $20,000 to $25,000 per month puts you in the high-earner category in most courtrooms as this is written (2000). A colleague of mine presides, in part, over cases from Beverly Hills, where children of film and television stars and major sports figures are commonly transported in limousines and cared for by expensive, full-time nannies. He has stated in attorney-education programs that he is not certain that earnings of $1,000,000 per year puts you in the high-earner category in his courtroom!

If you are an obligated parent, a high earner, and live in a state in which the child support of a high earner will be determined by the needs of the child at the high earner's standard of living, consider this: *You could wind up paying more in child support than the guidelines would have imposed on you.* Before you claim that you are a high earner and that child support should be based upon the children's needs rather than set by guideline, be sure you earn enough so that support by schedule will be greater than support based upon need. Judges will not be stingy in determining the support needs of children of wealthy parents, and the award could be several thousand dollars per child.

Not all states set child support based upon need when the supporting parent is found to be a high earner. A substantial number of states have a maximum amount in their guidelines, and that amount is presumed to be what all high earners will pay in child support. In those states it is far less difficult to determine whether you should or should not claim to be a high earner. Indeed, you may have no choice. If you earn more than the supporting parent at the highest state guideline figure for child support, you are automatically classified as a high earner.

Finally, you should be aware that some states apply an entirely different child support formula for high-earner cases than the one they use for ordinary earners.

Unemployed by Choice — "Really Lazy" Parents

All states will permit judges to "attribute" or "impute" a fictitious income to a parent who refuses to be employed. For example, if an obligated parent quits a job so as to avoid paying child support, the judge will simply "impute" the income that *could* be earned, according to the parent's work history.

Consider the parent who remarries someone of substantial income and simply decides to be a homemaker as a matter of lifestyle. In states where the judge cannot consider new-mate income, imputed income may be the only reasonable solution. If that person is the noncustodial parent, there is no income from which the judge could order child support unless the judge imputes income to that parent. If that person is the custodial parent, unless some income is imputed, then the noncustodial, supporting parent will pay an unreasonably high level of child support because all of the support would have to come from the supporting parent alone.

Multiple Families — The Battle for Dollars

All states allow judges to consider other children of prior relationships that either the obligated parent or the payee parent must support. The struggle for a parent's dollars, between that parent's prior family and current family, is one of the ongoing dilemmas of child support law. There are no easy solutions. The judge must consider the needs of all the children a parent is obligated to support, not just those in the case now before the court. If the obligated parent has two children of a prior — or new — relationship to support, that parent will not be able to pay as much for the children for which the court is setting support. Likewise, if the payee parent is raising two other children of another relationship, only a portion of that parent's earnings will be available for the children in the case before the court. Thus it may be appropriate that the paying parent pay less or more child support, based upon one of the parent's obligations to support children of another relationship.

The exact method by which a judge can consider the obligations of parents for their children of other relationships varies from state to state, but in general we can say that the funds needed to support the children of another relationship are deducted from the income of the parent supporting those children, and the child support schedules are applied to the lower income level created by the deduction. In a minority of states, the existence of other children needing support allows the judge to deviate downward from guideline support.

However, the truth is that when we deal with children of other relationships, the variables are more complex than the general rule in the preceding paragraph reveals. There are actually three different situations. *First,* there are the children of another relationship who are living with the parent who is a party to the case. *Second,* there are the children of another relationship who are not living with a party to the case but for whom a party is paying child support. *Finally,* the children in the two groups just described will be in one of two other categories: they will either be *born before* the children of the case before the judge, or *born after* the children in the case.

The vast majority of states defer to prior child support orders by permitting the judge to deduct payments for the children of prior relationships (born before) from the gross income of the paying parent. Many states will allow a deduction for the cost of raising a child of a prior relationship that is living with the parent. In a minority of states, support obligations for children of prior relationships are treated as a factor that allows the judge to deviate downward from guideline support.

Many states, however, treat the children of *subsequent* relationships (born after) differently than they treat children of *prior* relationships. For example, if we assume a father had two children with mate number one, was divorced or separated, and has now had two children with new mate number two, the children of the second relationship are treated differently by many states. This discrimination is related to the public policy that discourages parents from taking on additional support obligations to the detriment of children already in need of support. For example, if mate number one makes a motion to establish or increase child support, not all courts will allow a deduction from gross income of the father for the cost of raising the two subsequent children now living with him. A few courts make the deduction mandatory. Three states make a deduction from gross income at the judge's discretion. The majority of states allow the judge discretion to deviate from guideline support.

There is a small trend in some states to try to treat all of the children of a supporting parent equally. That is, the amount that the judge deducts from the parent's income, as a result of that parent's duty to support a child of another relationship, will be no greater than the amount of support that will be awarded to a child in the case before the judge. I am uncertain of the extent to which judges with the discretion to do so follow this concept. In California, equality is mandated unless there is a court order for children of other relationships, in which case that order is deferred to regardless of what the level of support will be in the case before the judge.

Finally, I know of no state that allows a judge to deviate from guideline because one of the parents before the court has stepchildren in the home. The rationale is that the parent has no legal duty to support stepchildren; these children should be supported by their birth parents.

Parent Expenses and Child Support

One similarity among all state guidelines is that a parent's expenses are irrelevant in determining the guideline support figure. Expenses are considered discretionary and are to be reduced if necessary in order that paying parents can meet their support obligations. The protection of the obligated parent's standard of living was not the goal of any state legislature in passing laws establishing child support schedules.

Health Care and Medical Expenses

Almost all states provide for the payment of unreimbursed health care costs as a form of child support. These are normally equally divided or apportioned in the ratio of the parents' incomes. In almost all states, these payments are in addition to child support set by schedule. A few states allow the judge to deviate upward from guideline support to provide for payment of unreimbursed medical expenses. This would seem to be an unsatisfactory system because the judge is required to speculate on what yearly unreimbursed medical expenses will be in the future when determining how much to increase guideline support. An order that each party contribute a given percentage of whatever the expense may turn out to be would seem preferable.

Health insurance costs are primarily treated in two ways. They are added to a guideline child support award or they are a deduction from income.

Child Care Expenses

As with uninsured health care costs, most states order the cost of work-related child care expenses to be paid in addition to the figure that is determined by the guidelines to be presumed correct. Most states require the judge to apportion child care expenses between the parents; the supporting parent's share is added to guideline child support in the same way that unreimbursed medical expenses are added.

Here's a hypothetical example:
- child support schedules call for support of $500 per month for one child;

- day care provider charges are $400 per month;
- day care charges are to be equally divided;
- the obligated parent will pay $200 for day care and $500 in child support, bringing the total to $700 per month.

Some states make day care expenses a factor that allows the judge to deviate from schedule by increasing guideline support so that the cost of day care is equitably shared. Finally, six states allow the party paying child care expenses to deduct that sum from gross income. This usually has the effect of decreasing the supporting party's guideline child support so as to make funds available with which to pay day care expenses.

Assigning Wages for Support

All states have laws that mandate or permit child support to be paid by wage assignment, often called an "earnings withholding order." A court order is served upon the employer of the obligated parent requiring the employer to pay child support directly to the payee parent or to a public agency which in turn remits the funds to the parent receiving the support. It is no longer a stigma to have your employer served with such a wage garnishment for child support. Most employers just consider it to be an obligation that comes with the hiring of employees. Employers know that a wage assignment no longer indicates that the employee is behind in support payments. Starting in 1998, federal law requires employers to honor wage assignments from courts of other states just as if they were issued in the state where the employer company is located. If the employer fails to properly respond, the local court will be required to enforce the wage assignment from the other state.

What Are We Fighting About?

Child support disputes are virtually always about the facts of the case, seldom about the schedules or how to use them. Disputes concern whether the parents are disclosing all of their income, and center on questions such as these: Is the corporation employing one parent paying personal expenses of that parent and thus concealing extra income? Does one parent receive cash for work that is never reported to the IRS or the court? More sophisticated disputes might raise these questions: Does a family-owned business retain earnings that could be paid in salary to one parent? Was a loan by the business to the employee-parent actually salary disguised as a loan, to avoid both withholding taxes and increased child support?

In those states that consider the sharing of time as a factor in setting child support, the major dispute is often over what percentage of time each parent has the children. Parents arrive in court with elaborate calendars and charts. Some parents want to count hours rather than days, or exclude from consideration the hours in which the child is asleep or in day care, or count a midweek visit from 3 to 6 p.m. as half a day. Most judges will not become involved in counting hours, or excluding sleep and day care time from consideration, but will simply make an approximation of the time-share by looking at the overall pattern of visitation.

Time sharing is so important in those states that consider it in setting child support because it can make a huge difference in the amount of support paid. Here's an example: the obligated parent earns $6,000 gross per month and the payee parent earns $4,000 gross per month, and the parents share equal time with three children; in California, child support is $265 per month. If instead the obligated parent rarely sees the children — let's say his share of time is just 2 percent (less than one day a month) — child support is $1,854 per month, seven times as much as in the equal time share.

The Attitude of Judges Toward Child Support Schedules

Family court judges are generally quite hostile to mandatory support schedules and formulas. They see such mandates as a limitation on their freedom and ability to do justice in any individual case by looking at the particular facts of the case. They look upon the schedules in the same way that federal and state criminal court judges look upon mandatory sentencing laws: a one-size-fits-all approach that is harmful to any effort to do justice.

I, too, have often wished for greater latitude to make my ruling fit the needs of an individual case. However, I am strongly supportive of mandatory child support schedules. Up until the introduction of such schedules, the amount of child support that was awarded to custodial parents was woefully inadequate and certainly not in the best interests of children anywhere. Judges tended to concentrate too much on the bills and debts of the payers — normally dads — and not enough on the needs of children. When judges looked at dad's expenses and said to the mother, "Ma'am, there's just not enough money to go around," that meant, "You and the children are going to live in poverty, at a level far below the marital standard." And this scene repeated itself over and over again, because if the judge looks at the payer's income-less-expenses, there is almost never enough money to go around. Only by the use of schedules have we been able to require judges to look exclusively at income. Schedules say to the judge and the payer, "Living expenses are discretionary. If you have to obtain cheaper housing, drive an older car, or eat out less to be able to pay child support, then do so." Schedules say to payers, "This is the amount of child support you must pay based on the earnings of you two parents. Now you must adjust your lifestyle so that you can pay that sum." This new approach, with the use of mandatory schedules, has meant that for the first time mothers have enough money with which to raise their children decently.

It is this judge's considered opinion that children in our society have greatly benefited from the use of child support schedules by the courts.

DO'S AND DON'TS

Do . . .

• Be sure that you understand exactly how child support levels are determined by judges in your state. Are child support schedules mandatory? When can the judge depart from them? Is the amount of time spent with the children a factor in setting child support in your state? If so, how? It is your attorney's job to explain all of this to you in a way that you can understand.

• Obtain a copy of the child support schedules or work sheets that are used by the court in your jurisdiction. If you are in California, sit with your attorney in front of her computer while she enters the data into the child support program and the results are calculated. Enter the facts as you believe them to be and as the other parent believes them to be. Realize that the judge's ruling will likely be somewhere in between.

• If you suspect that the other parent is deliberately refusing to be employed or to work to capacity, ask the judge to impute income to that parent based on past earnings. If the other parent has been a homemaker for many years so that there is no reliable record of past earnings, ask the judge to order a vocational evaluation of the other parent.

• Learn how the children of another relationship you are legally obligated to support will affect the child support you are required to pay for the children in the case before the judge.

• When you receive an award of child support in a case in which the obligated parent is an employee, immediately obtain a wage assignment from the judge and serve it on the employer. If the obligated parent is self-employed, you may wish to ask the judge to order that parent to post security to insure the payment of child support.

Don't . . .

• Don't expect child support to be timely and fully paid if you are thwarting the relationship of the children with the other parent. Parents willingly pay support for children with whom they feel a close relationship. (Review the statistics on page 134.)

• Don't forget that in some states the amount of time you spend with a child may have a gigantic impact on the amount of child support you receive or are required to pay.

• Don't think that a plea of "I can't afford it" to the judge will result in a reduction of child support below the level required by the child support schedules.

• In those states where the child support of "high earners" is based on the needs of the child, don't claim that you are a high earner and can pay whatever the judge determines are the reasonable needs of your child unless you are sure that support based on needs will be less than what the guidelines would require you to pay.

• Don't let the other parent claim that the judge should reduce that parent's child support based upon the duty to support children of another relationship, unless that other parent is actually paying the support. Insist on seeing canceled checks for the past year or so.

• Don't expect a reduction in the child support you pay because you have stepchildren living with you.

• Don't pay your attorney to put on a "dog-and-pony show" in court, with charts and calendars on the issue of time-sharing, unless you have some reason to believe that the judge will be interested in an effort to micro-analyze the parenting plan.

• Don't believe that children have not benefited greatly from mandatory child support schedules.

13.

Attorneys and Fees in Custody Litigation

n any legal proceeding, you are almost always better off with an attorney than without one. A capable and experienced attorney is a valuable resource and can enhance a parent's chances for a favorable ruling. In a custody case, a capable attorney will explain to you, in advance, what you should expect at each step in the process of arriving at a custody award or settlement, and will also give you valuable advice on how to conduct yourself. If your anxieties are allayed, you will likely appear more relaxed and confident and will make a better impression on the custody evaluator.

How Much Will It Cost?

A full-blown custody battle ending in a trial of a day or so can cost each party from $35,000 to $100,000. A custody dispute that settles after a recommendation by a court-appointed expert in the needs of children will probably cost no more than $10,000 to $20,000 for each party. These figures include the fees of attorneys and other experts involved in the *custody* litigation. Not included are attorney fees and costs that will be incurred in hearings on *child support* or the *division of property*. If the parties are relatively well off and the high earner is self-employed, a CPA may be required, to determine the income from the business that will be available to the high earner for support payments. Thus, in addition to a cost of $35,000 to $100,000 for the custody portion of the case, the parties may well spend a like amount in the litigation of financial issues.

Do I Really Need an Attorney in a Custody Case?

It is your author's opinion that attorneys have less influence on the outcome of a custody issue than they have on other aspects of divorce litigation. In most jurisdictions, the custody evaluator will listen to the attorneys for each side, well aware that each description has a spin in favor of the parent that the attorney represents. After this initial summary, the attorney's direct involvement in the custody case is rather limited. The custody evaluator is far more interested in talking to the parents and watching them interact with their children than in listening to a biased account of the issues.

These remarks are not intended to be critical of attorneys. Indeed, they are under an oath to present their client's case in the best possible light. Moreover, if your attorney's reputation with the judge and custody evaluator for candor and integrity are unblemished, the summary of the case will have great weight with the evaluator. But the core of a custody case for the evaluator is the needs of the children. The evaluator is not apt to be captivated by an attorney's rhetoric, no matter how well regarded the attorney may be. The parents and the children are the keys to a recommendation that will be in the best interests of the children. If the children are preteen or older, it is likely that their own views will be far more important to the evaluator than the opinion of either attorney. On the other hand, if an attorney has been appointed by the judge to represent the children, the evaluator will take a great interest in the views of that attorney, especially if the attorney is one with a reputation for good judgment and insight. Unlike the attorneys for the parents, the children's attorney will be seen as an impartial and insightful witness in the case.

Should You Be Your Own Attorney?

There are advantages and disadvantages to self-representation. If you do proceed *in pro per* (or *pro se*), and if you are the parent to whom the children are more closely bonded and your conduct in raising the children has been appropriate, an attorney for the other parent will not be able to derail an award of custody that is favorable to you. However, you should inform yourself about the court process in custody cases in your jurisdiction. This book is a good beginning, but each jurisdiction may have local rules of procedure that differ from other jurisdictions. A copy of local rules should be available to you at minimal cost at the courthouse or nearby.

Of course, self-representation can save a great deal of money. Indeed, some *pro per* parents deliberately prolong the process so as to drive the *represented* parent into insolvency. Judges and evaluators, however, are not impressed with this tactic and it can only hurt your case. In addition, if a *pro per* brings a series of meritless motions, in most jurisdictions that parent can be found by the judge to be a "vexatious litigant." When that occurs, the litigious parent is required to post a bond to secure payment of the other party's attorney's fees prior to filing any motion, or is required to have a judge's permission before a motion can be filed, or both.

Will Fees Be Awarded to the Low Earner?

Most judges feel a commitment to maintaining a level playing field in all aspects of a divorce case, including custody disputes. The lower-earning party can normally expect some assistance with attorney fees by an order from the judge requiring the higher earner to pay a portion of the fees and costs of the lower earner. A judge will likely award attorney fees to the low earner sufficient to allow the attorney to prepare a custody motion (or response to a motion) and to assist in preparing the client for the evaluation process.

But in custody cases, there is a cutoff point. Do not expect an award of attorney fees to allow you to attack the recommendation of the evaluator appointed by the court. If you wish to pay an attorney to locate, retain, and prepare a privately retained expert to take a position hostile to the judge's expert, do not expect to receive an award of fees and costs for this effort, and certainly don't expect to receive an award in advance. You will not likely even receive an award of fees to allow your attorney to take the deposition of the expert appointed by the judge. Of course, the chances of an award of fees to the low earner after a custody decision has been rendered will be greatly enhanced if the low earner prevails and establishes that the report of the neutral expert was indeed flawed.

Prevailing against the court's expert is rare, however, and any fee award would come after the case has been resolved. If you are the low earner, you should not expect your attorney to wait until the case is over to be paid. Most attorneys will refuse to do so. Thus, if you expect to be represented by an attorney in these latter stages of a custody case, you must find a way to keep your attorney's bill current.

On the other hand, you may be required to defend an attack on the court's expert who has made a recommendation in your favor. In this event, if you are the low earner, you can expect an award of attorney fees in advance, and perhaps an additional award of fees if the decision is rendered in your favor.

A low earner who wishes to change attorneys will not likely receive an award of fees for a second retainer, especially after receiving an adverse recommendation from the neutral expert or an adverse interim ruling from the judge. The judge will see you as just another litigant who judges the attorney's work by the results achieved, as if the attorneys created the facts with which they must work. The judge has, over and over, seen attorneys fired after adverse rulings or recommendations, and the judge almost always believes that such conduct is misguided and contrary to the best interests of the children. Indeed, sacking your attorney after an adverse recommendation can affect your chances of a favorable custody ruling if the judge believes that it reflects your poor judgment and temperament.

If you are the low earner, you may reasonably expect an award of costs to pay for a court-appointed therapist for the children. Or the judge may simply order the higher earner to pay a larger portion of the therapist's fees. However, you will not receive an award of fees if the court suspects that you are seeking a therapist to be an ally in the litigation rather than to engage in actual treatment of your child.

The low earner may also reasonably expect that the high earner will be ordered to pay a greater proportion of the fees of an attorney appointed for the children. However, this will not be done if the attorney for the children conveys to the judge that most of the attorney's work was required by the misconduct of one parent. That parent may be ordered to pay all or most of the attorney fees, regardless of the relative earnings of the parties.

Thus, in a custody dispute, the low earner can reasonably expect an award of fees for the work of an attorney up to the completion of the custody report and recommendation of the evaluator. However, once the opinion of a neutral and qualified evaluator has been rendered, it is unlikely that a low earner seeking to overturn the recommendation will receive financial help from the judge. On the other hand, an award of fees to the low earner to defend against the onslaught of "guns" hired by the high earner is likely to be quite generous, especially if the low earner needs funds to defend the recommendation of the court-appointed neutral expert from attack by experts hired by the high earner.

DO'S AND DON'TS

Do . . .

• If you can afford an attorney to represent you, by all means hire one.

• If you are the low earner, in many states you can rely on an award of attorney fees if you and your attorney conduct your case in an appropriate way. In fact, an award of attorney fees may be made to you early on in the case, well in advance of most of your attorney's work.

• Keep current in payment of your attorney's bills if you want to have a good relationship with your attorney.

• If you are the low earner and are called upon to defend an attack by the high earner on the recommendations of the court-appointed custody evaluator, you can reasonably expect an award of attorney fees, especially if you are successful.

Don't . . .

• Don't conclude that because you cannot afford an attorney that you will be denied a just result that is in the children's best interest.

• Don't expect an award of attorney fees in order to attack the findings and recommendations of the court-appointed custody evaluator. However, if you are successful in showing that the work of the evaluator was flawed, then you might receive such an award.

Glossary

bailiff: Person in the courtroom whose primary responsibility is to assure the safety and security of everyone who enters. Often a deputy sheriff, but need not be. Courts in which the chance of a violent outburst is extremely remote may have a *court attendant*, who does not carry a firearm, rather than a bailiff. Family court is more prone to violence than any other division of the court, including the criminal division.

bonding: Process of a parent and child developing a strong positive emotional connectedness, usually beginning in infancy, and assuring that the parent's caretaking responses will occur. Bonding between an adult and an infant is the first step in the development of the essential *attachment* process, in which the child moves from total dependency on the adult to a sense of individuality. It is through this process that human values such as concern and empathy are communicated from one generation to the next. Individual differences in the attachment relationship influence the various traits, tendencies, and behaviors that will make up a child's personality as an adult.

bonding study: An evaluation performed by a mental health professional to determine the type and degree of relationship between the child and his or her parents or caretakers.

challenge for cause: Request for a judge or juror to step down from the case for stated reasons, which must be proven. The reasons ("causes") for which a judge or juror must step aside are set forth by statute in each state.

children's shelter: County facility that provides temporary group housing and care for abandoned, neglected, or, on occasion, "out of control" children.

children of prior relationships: Children of one of the parent-litigants from another relationship born *before* the children in the case now at court. For example, the father has children of a former marriage.

children of subsequent relationships: Children of one of the parent-litigants from another relationship born *after* the children in the case now at court. For example, the mother remarries and has another child.

custody evaluator: Person who evaluates a child's best interests and recommends to the judge a parenting plan for the child that apportions time between the separated parents. Often called a *custody investigator* or *custody assessor*.

custody investigator: See *custody evaluator*.

deposition: Process by which a party or a witness is questioned under oath by the attorney for the other party (or by the other party, if *in pro per*) prior to a hearing or a trial. The purpose usually is to determine what the person's testimony will be at the later hearing or trial.

discovery: Process of required disclosure of each party's contentions, facts, evidence, witnesses, documents. *Discovery* is a catch-all term that includes depositions, interrogatories, requests for admissions, and requests to produce documents or things.

divorce mill: As used in this book, a law practice in which the attorney of record (with whom you interviewed and who you retained to represent you) does not prepare the case for trial or any hearing. All discovery, witness interviews, and expert retention are accomplished by paralegals or underling attorneys. Your attorney seldom sees the file until the day before or evening before a hearing or trial.

ex parte **order:** Emergency order made without a hearing before a judicial officer. It may be made with or without notice to the other parent. It is effective only until a hearing before a judge (which is normally set when the *ex parte* order is made) can be held.

faking good: Process by which a person taking a psychological test answers questions untruthfully in order to try to appear more emotionally healthy. In particular, a person may give answers that present a distorted picture. The tests most widely used have questions designed to detect if a person is "faking good."

family court: Separate county facility for family law cases, or a group of judges who do exclusively family law work. Many jurisdictions do not have a family court, especially smaller jurisdictions where one or two judges will preside over all cases that are filed in the county. Some larger counties may have a judge or commissioner who hears all family law motions, but trials are assigned to any judge available; that is not normally considered a "family court."

gender bias: Favoring one litigant over another because of the litigant's gender.

guideline child support: Amount of child support set by a formula in each state, which yields a figure that is presumed to be correct. If judges wish to depart from that figure, they must explain their reasons on the record or in writing, and the departure must be sanctioned by statute.

hidden agenda: Unrevealed motive for continuing in litigation, such as to vent anger, hurt the other parent, or obtain personal approval or vindication.

imputed income: Income that a parent does not actually receive but that the judge attributes to that parent because the judge finds that the parent could or should earn or have that income. For example, a parent who refuses to seek employment may have income imputed by the judge.

interrogatories: Written questions by one party to the other, or to a witness, that must be answered under oath in writing. Like a deposition, interrogatories are said to be a means of *discovery*.

joint custody: Parenting plan in which each parent has significant time with the child. Often used improperly to mean an equal (50%–50%) sharing of time, excluding any other percentage arrangement. A 55%–45% or 60%–40% apportionment may also be considered joint custody in many jurisdictions. Synonymous with *shared custody*, a preferable term.

judicial officer: Broad designation to include a judge or commissioner, or a referee or special master appointed by a judge or commissioner.

legal advisor: As used herein, an attorney who advises a litigant and appears with the litigant in court, but who does not present the case. (The litigant presents the case.)

legal custody: The right to make parenting decisions for a child concerning education, religious training, health care, etc. If legal custody is joint, this authority is equally shared.

MCMI-3: Millon Clinical Multiaxial Inventory, third revised edition. A 175-question written questionnaire. Like the MMPI-2, the MCMI-3 is used by psychologists to help assess personality traits and diagnose personality disorders.

mediation: Process by which a third party seeks to bring adverse parties to an agreement on issues in dispute. *There is no ruling or decision by a mediator.*

mediator: Third-party facilitator in a mediation. The mediator's role is to bring the parties to a mutually agreed settlement, not to rule or decide the issues.

mental health professional: Catch-all designation used in this book to refer to psychiatrists, psychologists, marriage and family therapists, and licensed clinical social workers.

MMPI-2: Minnesota Multiphasic Personality Inventory, second revised edition. A written questionnaire of 567 items, originally developed in the 1930s and used very widely in psychological evaluations and research studies. The most commonly used of psychological tests, the MMPI-2 produces a personality profile and assessment of psychological functioning.

muscle mediation: Process by which a mediator serves not only to bring the parties to an agreement but, if the parties fail to agree, is empowered to recommend to the judge a permanent parenting plan based on information gathered during the mediation.

nesting arrangement: Custody plan, normally temporary, wherein the children remain in the same house and the parents move in and out, commonly on a weekly or bi-weekly basis.

paralegal: Person who has limited legal training to do research, prepare pleadings, and organize a case or hearing or trial under supervision of an attorney-employer. The paralegal is not a licensed attorney and cannot participate in a court hearing except as an assistant who locates documents, takes notes, etc., as the case is presented.

parental alienation: Process by which one parent makes a serious effort to estrange a child from the other parent, often by manipulating the child to fear, distrust, or be antagonistic to the other parent. The alienating parent may be acting on distorted perceptions, and therefore believe that such action is justified.

parental alienation syndrome: Characteristics exhibited by a child who has been, or is being, alienated or turned against one parent by the other. This is not a recognized diagnostic syndrome, but a collection of behaviors. While some estrangement is to be expected in almost any dissolution conflict, this syndrome shows a pattern of significantly negative behaviors, indicating damage to the child's mental health.

parentified: Characteristic of assuming some of the responsibilities of parenting, usually by a child. Often used to describe a child who experiences and acts on the responsibility for a parent's feelings, protecting that parent and keeping that parent from negative behaviors (drinking, anger, despair, impulsive acts). On occasion, "parentified" is used to describe a child who has an unusually strong sense of duty to protect and care for siblings, has reversed roles with a parent, and seeks to protect and care for the entire family.

parenting plan: Structured plan of custody and visitation or shared custody normally ordered by the judge, but often agreed upon by the parties.

peremptory challenge: Challenge to a judge or a juror for which no reason need be given and after which the judge or juror must step down from the case and a new judge or juror will be selected. Not all states permit a peremptory challenge of a judge, and those that do permit litigants only one peremptory challenge of a judge.

permanent child support: Child support awarded at or after trial of the case. It remains an order until modified by the court or until the child becomes an adult under the law of the state.

permanent custody award: Award that remains until changed by the court based on a change in circumstances or the agreement of the parties. The award is said to be "until further order of the court."

personality disorder: Collection of long-term deviant personality traits and behavior patterns that interfere with the person's functioning in personal, social, and/or work relationships. Such disorders can range from mildly disabling to very serious. Examples: extreme dependence on another person (often regardless of harmful behavior by the other); such self-focus that the person cannot perceive or act on the needs of others; disregard for the mores of society; dramatic overreactions; extreme gullibility; marked suspiciousness and inability to accept responsibility for one's life situation. Personality disorders are coded by the *Diagnostic and Statistical Manual of Mental Disorders* of the American Psychiatric Association, fourth edition, revised. Psychological evaluation and testing is used to diagnose personality disorders which may impact parenting ability.

primary custodial parent: Parent with whom the child spends most of the time. In shared or joint custody plans, neither parent is the primary custodial parent.

primary nurturing parent: Parent who has taken the greater responsibility in meeting the child's emotional and physical needs. Since parents differ in nurturing capacity and may take different roles at different times, the primary nurturing parent may not always be the primary psychological parent, but is seen as such by the child in the vast majority of cases.

primary psychological parent: Parent to whom the child is more deeply attached, usually through the provision of day-to-day feeding, nurturing, structuring, and regulating during the first three years of life. Adults have different and varying capacities to foster attachment. (See also *bonding*.)

private custody evaluation: Evaluation performed by a mental health professional in private practice, or on contract with the court or county to do evaluations for a fixed fee, rather than a person working for the court or the county.

pro per / in pro per / in pro se: Litigant who represents himself or herself in court without an attorney.

projection: Term used to describe a psychological process in which one disavows his or her own unacceptable psychological characteristics, reads them into other people's conduct, and then reacts to others in a defensive manner.

psychological evaluation: Process, usually conducted by a psychologist, to determine the emotional makeup and components of a person's character or personality as these relate to that person's ability to parent children. The evaluation will reveal how the person deals with — and reacts to — others and the world. The evaluation usually, but not necessarily, includes psychological testing.

public custody evaluation: An evaluation performed by a person employed or appointed by the court or county.

retainer agreement: The fee agreement that, among many other things, officially hires an attorney and states how the retainer fee will be used against the work to be performed. It is normally signed when the retainer fee is paid and before the attorney begins work on the case.

retainer fee: A sum of money paid to an attorney before he or she commences work on the case. It is normally then applied to the attorney's hourly fee and court costs. Part or all of a retainer fee may be nonrefundable; however, such a provision may not be enforceable in a court of law.

Rorschach (ink blot) Test: "Projective" psychological test sometimes used to assess subtle and less conscious personality dynamics. Rests on the theory that one will project her or his own internal world view onto ambiguous stimuli such as amorphous ink blots. The Rorschach is considered more subjective a test than the MMPI-2 and MCMI-3 and may not be as well received by some judges.

shared physical custody: The child spends a significant amount of time with each parent. It may or may not be an equal sharing of time. It is usually thought that physical custody is *shared* when each parent has more than 40% time with the child.

special master: Called a *referee* in many jurisdictions, a *special master* is a person appointed by a judicial officer to do an investigation or hold hearings and make certain findings of fact, recommendations to the judicial officer, or rulings. A special master or referee for parenting issues makes recommendations or decisions on disputes between parents over what is in the welfare of the child. Normally such a special master on parenting issues cannot be appointed without agreement of the parties.

substitution of attorneys: Document signed both by the attorney and the client, and filed with the court, wherein the attorney either officially enters the case to represent the client or leaves the case in favor of another attorney or the client *in pro per*. The document is not signed by the judge in most jurisdictions, but when filed with the court, it either gives to the attorney, or relieves the attorney of, the duty to represent the client in that case.

supervised exchanges: Exchange of the children from one parent to the other is accomplished in the presence of a third-party supervisor. The visitation may then be unsupervised. The usual purpose of supervised exchanges is to prevent violence or verbal abuse by one parent or between parents and, by doing so, to protect the children from trauma and emotional harm. On a rare occasion, supervised exchanges may be used to insure that a parent is not under the influence of drugs or alcohol when the children are picked up or returned.

supervised visitation: All visits with the child are in the close presence of a third party. The supervisor may be a professional supervisor or a relative or friend of the parties. The purpose of supervision is to protect the child.

temporary child support: Support for a child that is awarded pending trial of the case and the judge's ruling.

temporary custody award: Award of custody made prior to the time that a trial or hearing can be held. The trial or hearing will determine which parent, if either, should be awarded *permanent* primary physical custody of a child. A temporary award is normally not intended to establish a status quo; that is, it should not influence the permanent award. The temporary award is often made before the long-term best interests of the child can be evaluated, and is usually intended to insure a child's safety or maintain an existing parenting plan temporarily until those long-term interests can be evaluated.

Thematic Apperception Test: Occasionally used psychological test based on the idea that the person tested projects his or her own world view onto ambiguous images. Various images of people and objects are shown, and the client is invited to make up a story. Like the Rorschach, not highly valued by some judges.

women's shelter: Residential living facility offering temporary refuge to women (with or without children) seeking to escape domestic violence — especially those who have no one with whom to live and no funds to rent a residence. Most of these shelters offer excellent legal advice and assistance and often provide "support persons" to accompany the abused woman to court.

Index

—A—

abduction, 60, 71, 95, 121
  to foreign country, 60
abuse
  allegations of, 80, 101
  begets abuse, 57
  of child, 9, 15, 26, 71, 84, 95, 99, 100, 106
    psychological, 100
    physical, 28, 37, 65, 96, 112, 115
      no justification for, 114
    sexual, 100
    spousal, 71, 95, 109, 112, 115
    verbal, 62, 65
    victims, 95, 97, 109
access, 15, 16, 42, 69, 73, 83, 122
  by abusive parent to child, 101
  by accused parent to child(ren), 103
  of child to parent, 27
  of father to child, 102
  of noncustodial parent to child(ren), 67, 68, 70, 98, 134

  of other parent to child, 7, 60, 64
  of spouse abusers to child(ren), 114
  telephone
    by parent to child(ren), 62
  termination of one parent's, 71
  to custody and psychological evaluations, 86
Adams, Steve, 92
affidavit, 14, 15, 16, 130
agreement to use private evaluator, 33
alcohol problems, 14, 15, 24, 25, 32, 33, 55, 62, 71, 78, 80, 101, 103, 110
alienating parent, 119, 120, 121
alienation
  of child, 56, 110, 118, 124
  parental, 80
alienation campaign, 8, 55, 62, 71, 102, 120, 121, 124
allergic child, 89
alternating weekends, 70
American Psychological Association
  ethical standards, 83

amnesia, 77
anger, 3, 29, 40, 59, 79, 88, 101
    at other parent, 77
    child(ren)'s suppressed, 56
anger management, 110, 112
anti-domestic violence organizations,
    114, 116
appearance, 24, 25, 78, 80, 82
appellate court
    California, 89
arrests
    police reports, 113
assignment system, 128
asthmatic child, 89
attached. *See also* bonded, 5
attorney, 1, 2, 12, 14, 15, 17, 19, 20, 34,
    36, 39, 40, 41, 42, 43, 44, 45, 46, 47,
    48, 49, 50, 51, 52, 63, 84, 85, 87, 106,
    122, 123, 124, 127, 128, 129, 131, 144,
    146, 151
    family law, 86
    changing, 50
    children's, 10, 11, 64, 83, 103, 104
        appointed by judge, 148
    copying correspondence to client,
        44, 51
    criminal, 103
    hides parent's warts, 40
    initial interview, 45, 51
    judgment of work, 150
    knows judge
        advice of, 18
    local, 12, 43, 45, 51, 85, 86
    need for, 148
    other parent's, 20
    pleadings, 44, 51
    rules of professional conduct, 50, 51
    stigma of changing, 49
    use as therapist improper, 44
    value of, 147
    withdrawal by, 50
        asking judge's permission, 50
    won't finance your case, 50

attorney fee
    retainer, 42, 48, 51
        nonrefundable, 43, 52
attorney fees, 147, 149, 151
    advance, 150
    award to low earner, 149
    children's attorney, 150
    cutoff point, 149
    for attempt to reverse *ex parte*
        order, 16
    in false accusation cases, 106, 107
    keep account current, 150, 151
    level playing field, 42, 149
    retainer, 46, 49, 52
    second retainer, 150
    to contest evaluator's report, 18
automobiles, 137

—B—

bailiff, 47, 113, 114, 115, 116
banker, 46
battered women, 109
be truthful, 75
behavior, 77, 81
    bizarre, 77
    impulse-control problem, 79
    negative, 78
    provocative, 41
    suicidal, 77
behavior modification classes, 111
belief system, 72, 105, 125
Beverly Hills, California, 137
bonded, 5, 27, 35, 76, 101
bonding
    parent-child, 134
bonding study, 76
boyfriend, 8
brainwashing, 120
breadwinner, 27, 126
Burgess, 91, 92, 93, 94, 95, 96

—C—

calendaring of cases
    assignment, 128, 129
    direct, 128
California, 63, 90, 93, 94, 115, 123, 126,
    135, 137, 140, 143, 144
California Administrative Office of
    Courts, 134
California Family Law Report, 92
California Supreme Court, 91, 93
caretaker, 26, 27, 28, 38, 56, 93
caring for children
    aspects of, 26
Carlson, 90, 91, 93, 94
certified family law specialist, 43, 48,
    51
challenge
    for cause, 131
    peremptory, 128, 129, 131
Charlottesville, Virginia, 134
child abuse, 9, 15, 26, 71, 84, 99, 100,
    106
    physical, 99
child care expenses, 141, 142
child custody, 1, 19, 67, 94, 112, 116,
    126, 133, 134
    equal time-sharing, 68
    international, 60
    jargon, 67
    visitation, 11, 29, 32, 55, 60, 61, 62,
        67, 70, 72, 76, 97, 101, 115, 120,
        121, 123, 134, 135, 143
child support, 56, 71, 117, 119, 120,
    133–147
    guideline, 136, 141, 142
    high-earner cases, 137, 138, 145
    how long payable, 136
    low-income cases, 136
    mandatory schedules, 143
    mathematical formula, 135
    multiple families, 139
    payment of, 120, 134, 142, 144
    recognition of prior orders, 140

    relationship to child custody, 133
    schedules, 134, 139, 141, 144
    state laws differ widely, 134
    subjects of dispute, 142
    time-sharing as factor, 143
    treating all children of a supporting
        parent equally, 140
    wage assignment, 142, 145
*Child Support Guidelines: Interpretation
    and Application*, 134
child's privacy, 84
child(ren)
    alienation of, 110, 118, 124
    best interests of, 17, 37, 58, 60, 72,
        90, 144, 150
    effects of inadequate support, 133
    emotional damage, 53, 55, 56, 103
    emotional well-being, 6
    favorite activity, 54
    freedom to grow, 7
    loyalty of, 7
    music and language lessons, 137
    needs of, 28, 148
    neglect, 14, 101
    neighborhood, 137
    of divorce, 53
    of other relationships, 139
    of prior relationships, 139, 140
    parental control of, 7, 8
    protecting in dissolution, 53, 54
    summer camps, 137
    values
        education and achievement, 133
    young, 13, 19, 69, 104, 127, 131
children of another relationship, 135
children of divorce, 56, 59, 64
children of prior relationships, 139,
    140
children of subsequent relationships,
    140
children's best interests
    emphasize in evaluation, 28
children's shelter, 8

Christmas Day, 70
client's conduct
    attorney's critique of, 50
clinical training, 34, 36
clinician, 80, 104
coaches, 35
college, 137
community attitudes, 99
complaints
    about other parent, 29
computers
    in courtroom, 135
confidentiality, 105
    therapist-child, 58
consent
    when required, 63, 95, 123
contact
    between parents, 71
    noncustodial parent's with
        child(ren), 56, 60, 67, 70, 72, 90,
        91, 116
    with both parents, 90, 93
control
    by intimidation, 29
    of your mental processes, 79
conviction records
    for abuse or battery, 113
costs
    of divorce cases, 42
    of transportation for child(ren),
        95

counseling, 104, 111, 120
    for abuse victims, 109, 116
    for child witnesses of spousal
        abuse, 112
    for child(ren), 28, 64
counselors
    victim or victim-witness, 104
court
    appellate, 91, 93, 130
    clerk, 47
    reporter, 47

court hearing, 44
Court of Appeal, 91, 92, 93, 130
courthouse security, 113
CPA (certified public accountant), 147
credibility
    concealing facts taints, 21
criminal attorney, 103
criminal court
    judges, 143
criticism
    by one attorney of other, 46
    by one parent of other, 15, 29, 38,
        54, 56, 80, 119
        balance, 29
cross-examination, 12, 40, 85
crying, 25, 37
custody
    battle, 81, 101
        potential cost, 42, 147
    case for, 1, 53
        orientation program, 120
    decisions, 1, 87
        how they are made, 5
    litigation, 1, 2, 3, 19, 39, 43, 46, 62,
        67, 82, 85, 117, 147
    primary custodial parent, 28, 60, 67,
        69, 89, 91, 92, 93, 94, 97, 98, 105
    trial, 2, 18, 46
custody agreement
    parenting plan, 2, 3, 6, 10, 12, 14, 23,
        24, 27, 28, 57, 63, 67, 68, 73, 84,
        92, 94, 97, 119, 120, 134, 146
custody award
    permanent, 17, 117
    temporary, 13, 20
        should not be presumed
            permanent, 17
custody dispute
    potential cost of, 2, 42
    not gender-neutral, 3
    most important person to
        persuade, 12
    never call child as witness, 21

custody evaluation
  be truthful, 32
  interviews with children, 10
  interviews with parents, 10
  no right of confidentiality, 82
  private
    evaluator fees, 34
  promptness, 37, 87
  report, 151
  resembles arbitration, 24
  reveal abuse, 27, 112, 115
custody evaluator, 2, 3, 5, 10, 18, 21, 23,
  24, 33, 43, 45, 50, 58, 62, 63, 64, 69,
  72, 77, 78, 80, 83, 86, 98, 104, 112,
  113, 119, 120, 121, 122, 123, 147, 148,
  151
  agreed upon by the parties, 13
  has greatest impact on case, 20
  neutral, 12, 13, 18, 21
custody law, 43
custody of child(ren), 1, 19, 60, 67, 94,
  112, 116, 126, 133, 134

—D—

day-care providers, 11
declaration, 43
  in *ex parte* custody hearings, 13, 14,
    15, 50
deduction from income, 141
delusions, 62
dependency
  financial and emotional, 109
dependency proceedings, 71
deposition, 149
depression, 77
deputy sheriff, 114
detrimental acts, 101
diaper rash, 32
discharge
  of attorney, 49, 52
discipline, 26
discovery, 44
dissolution action. *See also* divorce, 95

district attorney, 96, 129
diversion programs, 110
divorce, 3, 9, 13, 35, 41, 42, 43, 53, 56,
  88, 102, 125, 148, 149
divorce mill. *See also* Glossary, 44, 52
documentary proof, 115
domestic violence, 80, 100, 109, 110,
  112, 114, 115, 116
  counseling, 111
  false recanting, 110, 116
  rehabilitation treatment, 112
  victim's testimony needed, 111
drawings, 81
dress. *See also* appearance, 24, 25, 37,
  75, 78
driving under the influence, 32
drug use, 14, 15, 24, 25, 62, 71, 80, 101,
  110

—E—

earnings withholding order. *See* wage
  assignment, 142
Easter, 70
education
  importance of, 6
  parental, 120
emergency restraining order
  temporary, 111
emotional damage, 53, 55, 56, 103
  symptoms of, 56
emotional problems, 24
empathy, 82
employment
  refusing, 145
  work to capacity, 145
equal time-sharing, 68
evaluation
  psychological, 11, 24, 35, 36, 46, 55,
    75, 76, 77, 78, 79, 80, 81, 83, 84,
    85, 87, 88, 105, 106
  report, 84
  litigant's right to see reports, 88
evidence of abuse, 113

ex parte order, 13, 14, 15, 16, 21, 44
expectations
    attorney's of client, 46
    within family, 6
expenses
    child care, 142
    day care, 142
    health care
        unreimbursed, 141
    medical, 141
    of parent irrelevant, 141

—F—

failing in school. *See also* school
    grades, 8
faking good, 82
false allegation, 102
Family Code, 115
family court, 71, 77, 89, 104, 118, 126
    help centers, 111
Family Court Services, 113
family home, 41, 53, 57, 112
    order evicting abuser, 111
family law
    complexity, 43
family law attorney, 96
family law research, 134
family lawyer. *See also* certified family
    law specialist, 43, 48, 49, 51
family system, 81
fear, 58, 59, 72, 94, 117, 118, 127, 131
    child's of losing parent, 7
    for your safety, 97, 112, 116
    of harm to children, 15
    of judges that teens will disobey
        order, 8
    of parent by child, 32, 36, 102
    of reporting abuse, 109
    parent's, 79
feedback, 76
financial and emotional dependency,
    109
fishing expedition, 76

forensic
    experts, 13, 47, 51
    psychologist, 47, 51
forum shopping, 127, 130
foster care, 101

—G—

Garland, Judy, 78
gender bias, 125, 126, 127, 130, 131
group counseling, 64
group therapy
    for child(ren), 59
guardian *ad litem. See also* attorney
    for child, 46, 83, 103, 106
guidelines
    child support, 134, 135, 136, 138,
        141, 142
        maximum amount, 138
guilt, 59, 82

—H—

Hague Conventions
    on international child custody, 60
hairdresser, 46
hallucinations, 62
health care, 133
    unreimbursed costs, 141
hearing, court, 44
    on best interests of child(ren), 90
hidden agenda, 3, 11
    financial, 71
high earner, 42, 137, 138, 148, 150, 151
hired guns, 151
hired guns. *See also* Glossary, 13
HMO (health maintenance
    organization), 59
homemaker, 3, 126, 138, 145
homework, 6, 10, 26, 28

—I—

imputed income, 138, 145
in pro per, 148
in pro se, 39

in propria persona, 39
In re Marriage of Burgess, 91
In re Marriage of Carlson, 89
In re Marriage of McGinnis, 90
income
    business, 148
    deduction from, 141
    imputed, 138, 145
    of new mate, 136, 137, 138
indecisive, 81
independent counsel, 48
initial interview
    with attorney, 48
intelligence, 77
interim move, 94, 95, 96, 97
investigation, 62, 72, 90, 93, 102, 106, 107
Iran, 60
Israel, 60

—J—

jail sentences, 110
joint custody. *See also* Glossary, 5, 68,
    69, 72, 92, 93, 97, 126
    not gender-neutral, 69
judge, 2, 3, 5, 8, 9, 10, 12–25, 33–36, 40,
    41, 43, 46, 49, 57, 61–64, 68, 72, 73,
    77, 80, 83, 85, 86, 87, 90, 94–97, 99,
    101–104, 113, 114, 117, 119, 120–131,
    135–140, 142, 144, 145, 146, 148, 149,
    150, 151
    appointment of evaluator, 13, 34
    attitude of, 99
    discretion to deviate from guideline
        support, 140
    factors influencing in custody
        dispute, 13
    factors limiting actions, 101
    family court, 17, 101, 103
    sensitivity to issues of abuse, 110
    subjects of interest to, 39
    temporary custody hearing by, 14
judicial officer, 13, 25
juvenile court, 71, 101

—K—

Kaiser Permanente, 59

—L—

law enforcement, 32, 70, 103, 106, 111,
    114
legal advisor. *See also* Glossary, 41, 52
level playing field, 42, 149
Libya, 60
licensed psychologist, 35, 80
lien on your property, 48, 50
lifestyle, 81, 133, 138, 144
limits, 6, 8, 11, 25, 27, 31, 125, 128, 130
litigant, 40, 49, 113, 127, 150
    vexatious, 149
litigation
    of financial issues, 148
    paternity, 13, 90, 95, 117, 125
local attorney, 12, 43, 45, 51, 85, 86
look pathetic, 82
look sick, 82
look very good, 55, 82
love, 55, 57, 117
    for children, 29
    parent's, 6
low earner, 149, 150, 151
lying, 32

—M—

managed care organization (MCO), 59
marriage, failure of, 3
mature preteens, 30
McGinnis, 90, 93
MCMI, 81, 82, 85, 88
mediation, 2, 23, 24, 37, 45, 113, 114
    confidentiality of, 23
mediator, 23, 37
medical expenses, 141
men's groups, 69, 91, 93
mental health professional. *See also*
    Glossary, 3, 10, 16, 19, 20, 26, 33, 47,
    51, 54, 56, 61, 62, 63, 68, 86, 100, 114,
    118, 123, 124

metal detector, 113
Middle East, 60
midweek visits, 70
Millon Clinical Multiaxial Inventory-3,
    81
*Minnesota Multiphasic Personality
    Inventory II*, 81
MMPI, 81, 82, 85, 86, 88
molestation, 102, 103, 104, 105
    accusation, 35, 71, 102
    charge, 102, 103, 104
    false accusation, 56, 105
    steps to establish innocence, 103
Mom's House, Dad's House, 68
Morgan, Laura W., 134
    mother, traditional, 3
move-away cases, 35, 89, 92
    interim move, 94, 95, 96, 97
moving parent, 95
muscle mediation. *See also* Glossary,
    23

—N—

name-calling, 60
nannies, 137
narcissistic personality disorder, 82
National Law Research Group, 134
needy, 7, 26
neglect, 14, 101
    acts of, 100
nesting arrangement, 69
neutral evaluator, 12, 13, 18, 21
new mate, 11, 35, 57, 60, 71, 102, 118,
    140
new-mate income, 136, 137
nonrefundable, 43, 52
notification, 96

—O—

offers of proof, 40
one-way mirror, 11
orientation program, 120

—P—

Pakistan, 60
paralegal, 44, 46, 48
parent
    alienating, 119, 120, 121
    disordered, 3
    needy, 7, 26
    primary custodial, 89, 91, 94, 98
    primary nurturing, 5, 27, 126
    primary psychological, 5
parental alienation. *See also* Glossary,
    11, 36, 118, 119
parental education, 120
parentified. *See also* Glossary, 7
parenting, 31, 32, 57, 77, 85, 95, 101,
    119, 120, 123
    abilities, 37
    classes, 71, 101
    consistency, 6, 7, 8, 24, 25
    deficiencies, 29
    providing structure, 25
    setting limits, 6, 8, 11, 25, 27, 31,
        125, 128, 130
    shared, 68, 92, 94, 135
    skills, 2
parenting plan, 2, 3, 6, 10, 12, 14, 23, 24,
    28, 57, 63, 67, 68, 73, 84, 92, 94, 97,
    119, 120, 134, 146
    standard, 69, 70
    temporary, 27
parenting strengths list, 27
parents, 2, 5, 7, 8, 9, 16, 24, 25, 27, 28,
    36, 41, 42, 53, 57, 58, 59, 61, 62, 63,
    82, 83, 85, 90, 113, 117, 118, 120, 123,
    126, 143, 149
    advantages of agreement on
        private evaluator, 34
    attempts by teenagers to control,
        10
    belief that child needs two, 7
    conflict between, 6
    distrust of other parent, 55
    division of labor, 27

evaluation of, 11
improper conduct, 56
interviews with both, 19
judges' view of conduct, 59
both love child, 55
may be charged fee for public
    evaluator, 33
observation of, 11
psychological evaluation, 77
    of both in child molestation
    accusations, 105
role of, 58
separation of, 53, 57
vindictive, 54
witness-allies, 11
Parents United, 103
paternity, 13, 90, 117, 125
peremptory challenge, 128, 129, 131
permanent custody award, 17, 117
personal problems, 10
personality
    disorder, 3, 63, 76, 85, 87, 105
        narcissistic, 82
    structure, 2, 85, 86
physical abuse, 28, 37, 65, 96, 112, 114,
    115
    of child, 99
physical violence, 60
picking up your file, 51
pleadings, 44, 51
police
    changed attitudes about domestic
        violence, 109
police officer, 70
police reports, 80
polygraph test, 103, 106
poverty
    child(ren) raised in, 133
    threshold, 136
preteens, 5, 8, 10, 30
    importance of their views, 148
    mature, 30
    sexual harassment, 100

primary custodial parent, 28, 60, 67,
    69, 89, 91, 92, 93, 94, 97, 98, 105
primary nurturing parent, 5, 27, 126
primary psychological parent, 5
prior relationships, 140
private school tuition, 137
privilege
    confidentiality, 82
    therapist-child, 105
pro per, 39, 40, 41, 45, 50, 148, 149
pro se, 148
probation
    condition of, 112
probation reports, 80
procedural errors, 39
program, 30, 120
    treatment, 33
programming
    of child, 30, 38
proof, offers of, 40
projective tests, 81, 85, 88
prosecutor, 72, 115
    county, 96
protection, 97, 111
    domestic violence
        call police, 110
    for child(ren), 71
    of abused women, 109
    of child from parent, 61
provocative, 41
psychiatric evaluation, 77
psychiatrist, 36
psychological associations, 83
psychological evaluation, 11, 24, 35,
    36, 46, 55, 75, 76, 77, 78, 79, 80, 81,
    83, 84, 85, 87, 88, 105, 106
    of only one parent, 77
    private
        cost of, 36
        report, 84
psychological testing, 11, 27, 35, 76, 80,
    85, 88
    cost of, 76

psychologist, 36, 75, 76, 77, 78, 79, 80, 81, 82, 84, 85, 86, 87, 88, 106
  clinical observations, 79
  licensed, 35, 80
  privately retained, 87
  report, 80
  selectivity of, 86
psychotherapy, 82
  HMO attitudes toward, 59
public record, 84, 88
punctuality, 24, 75, 78

—Q—

questionnaires, 81

—R—

raw test data, 83, 86, 87
real property evaluation, 43
referee, 63
relationship, 6, 26, 29, 57, 120, 123, 130, 145
  attorney-client, 45
  between parents, 3, 12, 26, 77, 80
  child's, when adult, 56
  child(ren)'s with other parent, 54, 64
  child(ren)'s with parents, 84
  client-attorney, 151
  custody, 8
  of opposing attorneys, 45
  of parent with own parents and siblings, 79
  parent-child, 7, 11, 21, 30, 31, 35, 37, 61, 63, 79, 80, 81
  prior, 139, 140
  spousal, 111
  subsequent, 140
  with former partners, 79
relocation cases. See also move-away cases, 89, 90, 93, 94
reputation, 128, 129, 131
  of attorney, 43, 148
  of evaluator, 18
  of forensic psychologist, 19

restraining order, 80, 115, 116
  directed to abuser, 111
Rorschach ink blot test. See also Glossary, 81, 85
rules of evidence, 41
rules of procedure, 39, 149
rules of professional conduct, 50, 51

—S—

salesperson, 82
Santa Clara County, 59
schedules
  child support, 144
school, 133
  grades, 8, 9, 56
  private
    tuition, 137
  success in, 6
schoolwork, 69
second expert, 19
second opinion, 18, 19, 20, 21, 64
secrets, 118
  parent-child, 54, 64
self-support reserve, 136
separation, 9, 25, 53, 57, 58, 59, 64, 79, 90, 126
  reducing toll on child(ren), 57
settlement, 2, 5, 17, 20, 50, 86, 87, 88, 94, 97, 147
  conference, 44, 46, 49
  offer, 45
sexual abuse, 100
sexual misconduct
  with child, 99
shared parenting, 68, 92, 94, 135
shouting, 60
Silicon Valley, 137
special master. See also Glossary, 63, 64, 83, 123, 124
spousal abuse, 71, 109, 112, 115
spousal support, 136
spring break, 70
standard of living, 141

standard plan, 69, 70
state law
    may conflict with psychological
        association rules, 83
State of California, 90
status quo, 17, 102
stepchildren, 140, 146
stock option evaluation, 43
striking a child, 100
structure, 6, 7, 8, 24, 85, 125, 126
    for child(ren), 6
substitution of attorneys, 50, 51, 52
suicidal behavior, 77
summer camps, 137
supervised visitation, 61, 62, 71, 72, 76,
    115, 121
    by relative, 61
    fees, 61
support
    child, 71, 117, 119, 120, 133, 134, 135,
        136, 137, 138, 139, 140, 141, 142,
        143, 144, 145, 146, 147
support schedules
    mandatory
        judges dislike, 143
suspended visitation, 71
suspicious, 81

—T—

tape recording, 80
tax bracket, 137
tax law, 43
tax shelters, 135
teachers, 10, 11, 28, 35, 56, 84
tears. *See also* crying, 26
teenagers, 6, 7, 8, 9, 10, 30, 120, 124,
    133
    manipulating, 8
    sexual harassment, 100
    voting with feet, 7
telephone calls, 48
    failure to return, 44

temporary custody
    award, 20
    hearing, 46
temporary emergency restraining
    order, 111
temporary placement, 102
Tender Years Doctrine, 94, 127

test data
    raw, 83, 86, 87
testifying, 10, 115
    refer to "our" child, 33
testing
    psychological, 11, 35, 76, 80, 85, 88
Thanksgiving, 70
thematic apperception test, 81
therapist, 36, 58, 59, 83, 84, 103,122,
    123, 124
    child(ren)'s, 11, 28, 54, 55, 58, 62, 64,
        104–106, 150
        both parents should approve
            choice, 58
        should not treat either parent, 58
    fee-for-service, 59
traditional mother, 3
traits, 32, 81, 82
transportation expenses
    for child(ren), 95
    in relocation cases, 97
trial judge, 90, 92, 93, 96
trust
    ability to, 29, 41, 53, 120

—U—

University of California at San Diego,
    18, 25, 126
unreimbursed health care costs, 141

—V—

verbal reprimand, 100
vexatious litigant, 149
victims of abuse, 95, 97, 109

violence
    physical, 60
visitation, 11, 29, 32, 55, 60, 61, 62, 67,
    70, 72, 76, 97, 101, 115, 120, 121, 123,
    134, 135, 143
    supervised, 61, 62, 71, 72, 76, 115,
        121
    suspended, 71
vocational evaluation, 145

—W—

wage assignment, 142, 145
without prejudice, 18, 102

The Wizard of Oz, 78
women's groups, 69, 91, 93, 109, 114
women's shelters, 95, 109, 111, 116
work to capacity, 145
workload
    evaluator's, 12

—Y—

Yellow Pages, 48
young children, 5, 13, 19, 30, 69, 104,
    127, 131

MORE BOOKS WITH *IMPACT*

We think you will find these Impact Publishers titles of interest:

Cool Cats, Calm Kids
Relaxation and Stress Management
for Young People
Mary Williams, M.A.
Illustrated by Dianne O'Quinn Burke
Softcover: $8.95   32 pages

Guide to stress management for children 7-12. Uses "cats" as teachers, illustrating catnaps, stretching, "hanging in there." Includes section for parents, teachers, and counselors.

Teen Esteem: A Self-Direction Manual
for Young Adults (2nd Edition)
Pat Palmer, Ed.D., and Melissa Alberti Froehner, B.A.
Softcover: $9.95   112 pages

Written directly for teens, *Teen Esteem* helps build the attitudes and behaviors they need to handle peer pressure, substance abuse, sexual expression, with new material on ways to deal with anger. Includes illustrations.

"I Wish I Could Hold Your Hand..."
A Child's Guide to Grief and Loss
Pat Palmer, Ed.D.
Illustrated by Dianne O'Quinn Burke
Softcover: $8.95   32 pages

A best friend has moved away... Dad no longer lives with the family... A favorite relative or pet has died. This warm and comforting book gently helps the grieving child identify his or her feelings and learn to accept and deal with them.

Ask your local or online bookseller, or call 1-800-246-7228 to order direct.
Write for a free catalog.
Prices effective November 2001, and subject to change without notice.

Impact ✍ Publishers®
POST OFFICE BOX 6016
ATASCADERO, CALIFORNIA 93423-6016
Visit us on the Internet at www.impactpublishers.com

Since 1970 — Psychology You Can Use from Professionals You Can Trust